CW00566947

SACRED
RITUALS

Rev. Nóirín Ní Riain PhD is an Interfaith Minister (One Spirit Interfaith Seminary), an internationally acclaimed spiritual singer, theologian, writer, musicologist, and Celtic Spirituality expert. Rev. Ní Riain performs weddings, naming ceremonies, concerts, lectures, and gives workshops all over the world. She lives near Glenstal Abbey, County Limerick, Ireland.

SACRED RITUALS

A Simple Book of Everyday Prayer

Nóirín Ní Riain

HACHETTE
BOOKS
IRELAND

First published in Ireland in 2023 by
HACHETTE BOOKS IRELAND

1

Cataloguing in Publication Data is available from the British Library.

ISBN 9781399729468

Typeset in Adobe Garamond Pro by Cathal O'Gara
Printed and bound in Great Britain by Clays Ltd, Elcograf S.p.A.

Hachette Books Ireland policy is to use papers that are natural, renewable
and recyclable products and made from wood grown in sustainable
forests. The logging and manufacturing processes are expected to conform
to the environmental regulations of the country of origin.

Hachette Books Ireland
8 Castlecourt Centre
Castleknock
Dublin 15, Ireland

A division of Hachette UK Ltd
Carmelite House, 50 Victoria Embankment, London EC4Y 0DZ

www.hachettebooksireland.ie

CONTENTS

TÍOLACHADH : DEDICATION

I am writing this dedication on July 3rd, 2023, the Hindu, Jain and Buddhist festival of Guru Purnima. On this day, our teachers, spiritual and intellectual guides, mentors and gurus are honoured. This ritual book is dedicated to the muses in all our lives that, as poet Robert Frost would say, 'just gave you a little prod behind'.

RÉAMHFHOCAL:
FOREWORD

It is unusual, if not incautious, to find a book on prayer which shares the actual ways in which the author prays. Other books might tell you what prayer is, or how to set about it. This book takes you into the boiler room, the daily routines which have emblazoned the life of one who has been in communication with God since early childhood.

Nóirín Ní Riain is a singer. Song is her existence. Her voice is a gift from God, given to her as a child prodigy and which, like wine, has only improved with age. We typically presume that music is an entertaining way of using our voices, our bodies, our minds. Nóirín teaches us differently. Music is not a specialised case of a more basic non-musical existence. Music is the most fundamental conveyor belt of all experience; it is the way reality seeps into our blood stream. We may not realise it but music is our mother tongue: *Canto ergo sum*.

And prayer is the secret breath behind each note that Nóirín sings.

Which means also that this book cannot give you the real thing.

When Nóirín Ní Riain sings, it breathes an atmosphere of prayer which is contagious. People have been healed by her voice. While, as a printed word, this book cannot embody the magic of such singing, it can give the reader a compendium of rituals, prayers, evocations, and blessings, which she uses and has used all the days of her life. It also gives a flavour of how and where she found these aides and why they are important to her.

And this is as it should be. No one can teach us how to pray. Each of us finds that out for ourselves. If, as we are told, there are now eight billion people on our planet, then there must surely be eight billion ways of connecting with the Divine. Nothing really matters in this regard except your finding of the precise and practical way which allows you, first-person singular present tense, to make and maintain that vital connection. Until this happens, it is encouraging to read how others have found their way and established such a path.

Each of us is different and some accounts of prayer will resonate, while others will not. Some of her favourite prayers or preferred devotions may turn you off or leave you cold. That is the risk that love letters run when they stray into the public domain. The way we speak to those we love can sound ludicrous to some when overheard. The secret is to take what you find helpful and leave the rest. Not a book to read straight through as you might read a novel; rather a jewel box to open every now and then, allowing the Spirit to guide you to what suits yourself. Because the author, always in touch with 'the light from beyond the sea', is so trusting, so open-hearted and so bountiful, there is something here for almost everyone. Certain lines will sink deep into your solitude at the time you need them most.

Of this I am sure: the book you now hold in your hands is not an ordinary book. Nóirín is not entirely responsible for this happening. It was thrown to her as colours from the sky. Yes, she had to match it with enthusiasm and attach it gracefully to her loom; but hands other than hers worked gently by her side. Regard these pages, therefore, as sheet music. Give them your own live performance. Such co-operation alone can cause these buds to bloom.

> Had I the heavens' embroidered cloths,
> Enwrought with golden and silver light,
> The blue and the dim and the dark cloths
> Of night and light and the half-light,
> I would spread the cloths under your feet:
> **'He Wishes For The Cloths Of Heaven', W.B. Yeats**

Fr Mark Patrick Hederman,
former Abbot of Glenstal Abbey,
September 2023

RÉAMHRÁ:
INTRODUCTION

Today, many of us have lost and almost forgotten the art of mobilising everyday prayer and the Divine connection in our lives that our forebears understood instinctively and intimately.

We can regain this by marking the moments of our day with tiny practices that are bodily gestures towards the presence of the sacred in our lives, whether these are making signs of the cross, silently raising up our eyes or our hands, walking the earth thoughtfully or calling in the seasons. My aspiration for this book is to inspire you to find a new courage in life, in and through prayer and ritual. Because we are increasingly less grounded in religion, and perhaps in the rituals that once gave meaning and structure in our daily living, our innate yearning for the transcendent – the Other – longs to return and be rediscovered.

This prayer book was created out of my own personal practices through, as Yeats once said, the 'hollow lands and hilly lands' of my journey, sustaining me, keeping me going and helping me to explore more deeply who I really am. I believe that persevering in reading and returning to these sacred rituals here will do the same for you; the challenge, which you have already embraced, is to find your prayer space that you can revisit again and again through the touch of the page.

I never read an entire papal encyclical. But one morning I was wiling away the time and spotted an extract, *Laudato Si – On Care for our Common Home,* by Pope Francis, in a newspaper. A book about consumerism, environmental destruction and global warming, it was a No. 1 *New York Times* bestseller when it first appeared in 2015 and is an urgent cry for the world with an insightful cut and style. In that same newspaper, an article informed me that on the day that it was published, Pope Francis remarked to his advisers that global warming is 'a symptom of a deeper malaise'. True, Francis, very true. However, this disorder is a much broader, more complex issue. The demise of the holy in our world is the root cause. We have lost the run of our ritualistic selves and now we are paying the price. Honour yourself and your Higher Source and you will honour the planet in all its miraculous manifestations. Respect for life is the spirit of kindness to the earth.

In our global culture, where so much emphasis is put on materialism and individual ambition and success above community, compassion and contentment, rite and ritual can nourish and restore our spiritual and emotional selves.

It is also important that we retrieve this sacramental awareness from the jurisdiction of clerical supervision – we have to carry it back to the privacy of our own hearts. No one should have proprietary rights over where, when or how the grace of God manifests itself. The Spirit blows where the Spirit wills, and if any authority insists that this can only happen in a particular building, using specified equipment and precisely formulated arrangements of actions or words, then it has mistaken the fundamentals of prayer. There can be no limitation or restriction imposed on God's free movement in our world. No authority on earth can declare that your meeting with God is invalid because it does not conform to some set of arbitrary regulations. As the ancient wisdom of Psalm 118 advises: 'It is better to trust in God that to trust in humanity'.

There is no hierarchy among those on their knees. In other words, when we kneel together in a circle of prayer, we are all one and the same.

We have forgotten that deep prayer and meditation, which our troubled world needs so desperately now, must come from a source that includes the whole range of beliefs, including atheism, which is also a belief system. This offers very exciting possibilities and consequences, and it is my quiet hope, as a spiritual singer, that this prayer book may offer one possible 'hymn sheet' that we might all sing from in harmony.

Whatever your spiritual beliefs are at this moment – whether you have belonged to one faith that no longer serves you or whether you have belonged to none – read on.

You can pick up this compilation of prayers, looking for something particular to match your feelings – questions, doubts, gratitude, anxiety or elation – of the moment. The index may direct you to the right prayer for you. Or you may simply want to leave yourself open to the Law of Attraction, the philosophy which suggests that positive energy helps to manifest positive experiences. I am a great disciple of this form of energy. Believe in the positive and it will happen – it works the other way around too, so beware! Look for the negative and it will imprison you.

Your intention will lead you to the perfect prayer for you in the moment – you can't make a mistake or choose the 'wrong' prayer. Ask and pray for help as you hold this book and it will carry your personal intentions to the altar of a Higher Power. A ritual is also an act of intention – it is a moment and a space that we create to dedicate ourselves to prayer. A prayer ritual, as we will discover in this book, can involve reciting a prayer aloud, singing, or sitting in quiet contemplation – there are many ways to do it. And bringing this dedication into our daily lives, creating these special moments for prayer, will bring to us a greater sense of peace and a closer relationship to that which is greater than us.

However, before we define the terms 'ritual', 'prayer' and 'blessing', let me share some of my story with you, and how I came to view these three things as essential to my life.

The aspiration for this treasury is to guide you on your avenue to a freer soul destination. If you are searching for new beginnings through a more hope-filled reality, a deeper sense of purpose and personal self-esteem, you were meant to read this book!

A little aside here: keep a notebook and pencil nearby to jot down and make your own reflections that come to you as you read. There are also some spare pages at the end of this prayer book for you to do this. One thought, one new idea, is all it takes to inspire and be transformed.

MO SCÉAL FÉIN –
SCÉAL GACH DUINE:
My Story is Everyone's Story

As a young child, I fell in love with prayer. When I was six, my mother's sister, a nun, brought me a children's *Book of Prayer* that became my constant companion. I can still vividly remember the cover – a young girl kneeling and praying for the healing of, what seemed to me at the time, to be a very sick rabbit that she held to her heart. It was this gesture that enthralled me.

For many of us, the experience of prayer began at home. My father taught me, without either of us ever realising it, so much about prayer. This was his greatest gift to me. He was a good man who wanted to make a change in people's lives. I still, even now, hear new stories of how he reached out to the unemployed locals in our home village of Caherconlish, County Limerick, to give them jobs in the box factory he had founded. A successful businessman, the world of theology and scripture was a complete stranger to his day-to-day existence. I never saw him read a prayer book, not to mention the Bible.

It is so strange that as we grow older, our memories come to visit us full of presence and intimacy. As I think of my father in prayer, experiences of over sixty years ago surprise me. Every Sunday, I accompanied my parents to Mass. Although wedged in between them both in church, it was my father, on my right, who captured my attention. Mass, in the 1950s before Vatican II, was said predominantly in Latin. Da would produce his black rosary beads from his pocket for the duration of the service, oblivious to the ritual on the altar. His almost-audible whisperings would drown out what was, for me, the babble of the priest on the altar and I instinctively knew that this was doing him good, while for forty minutes or so, Da was in another world.

Then so many nights I watched him kneel beside his bed to say his own night prayers. Those three prayers – The Our Father, Hail Mary and Glory Be – were the stable elements that he held in and had off by heart.

That life of prayer came full circle before his death at the age of sixty. Every morning prior to his illness, he attended Mass in Limerick City, still praying on his black rosary beads

– his life-long ritual of reciting these well-known prayers never left him.

Two instances particularly are as pure, vivid, and intact as they were then. These lessons which I learned from my father carved my prayer practice and may also become meaningful for you.

I now see that, from then on, I became obsessed with sharing with others this power to transcend the material world, although I did not have then that language for the devotion. It started with my mother's hens. I loved them and pitied the lives they led. So, I decided that, if I could teach them to pray, it would be a great comfort and consolation to them, just as it was for me, a lonesome, awkward, uneasy child. This didn't go so well but even then, I was moved by the power of sharing and opening a spiritual space with others.

My teenage years were difficult and troubled. Convent boarding school, some three hundred miles from Caherconlish, a village in County Limerick in southwest Ireland, was not an easy ride; more roller-coaster than carousel. Auntie Mai, – the prayer-book gifter – lived on the campus, which was the reason I was sent so far away in the first place, though I was sometimes an embarrassment to her through my wayward behaviour and sullen personality. I did excel in singing, though, more because of training from the age of seven to twelve in Limerick city, than talent, and this went to my head! When I was sent off to boarding school, I was a very precocious, spoilt young girl, something that was cruelly stamped out when the reality of peer pressure appeared.

Largely because of this, friendships were in short supply during those years, and I lived in my own little world. It was miraculous to me that, thanks to my prayers, my heart did not freeze or congeal. *'Oh, that today, you would listen to God's voice, harden not your heart.'* (Psalm 50)

Prayer was my constant relief, and I spent many a solitary hour in the wooden gallery at the back of the school church, sharing my anxieties with the One whom I knew understood. I do not know how I would have survived without it. The weight of the world is very difficult for a young soul to bear. I carried the richness and the beauty of the prayers in my heart, and they kept me afloat when my whole being was turbulent and distracted with worry.

By contrast, my university days were halcyon – an idyllic, golden experience full of musical possibilities, an encounter with the love of my life and an unexpected linguistic treasure: a new love affair with the Irish language. All answers to my isolated teenage prayers. Married at twenty-three, Mícheál and I headed for An Rinn, the Waterford Gaeltacht to drench our souls in Gaeilge, the Irish language. Then a graced time in 1980 when I birthed two different blessings: our first son, Eoin, and the completion of a Masters in tradition religious song. The latter created our first relationship with the monks of Glenstal Abbey, our second home for many years after. My second son Mícheál, a further blessing, arrived four years later in 1984. In 1982, I visited India on the first of three cultural exchanges, representing Ireland as a musical performer, between the Irish Department of Foreign Affairs and the Indian Council for Cultural Relations. I immediately felt at home – it was a blessed time, and I have never been the same since. I learned so much about ritual, spiritual singing and prayer during my time there. That is where the seed for this book, however unconsciously, was sown. In the intervening years, I travelled the world, performing at events including the International Peace Gathering at Costa Rica to introduce the XIV Dalai Lama in 1989, the United Nations summit at Rio de Janeiro in 1992, the UN Earth Summit in Copenhagen in 1995 and the 40th Eurovision song contest that same year. I had the pleasure of singing with Sinéad O'Connor at the Royal Festival Hall, with saxophonist and band leader Paul Winter at summer and winter solstice concerts in the Cathedral of St John the Divine in New York, and with the Scola Gregoriana of Notre Dame University, Indiana. I also made several recordings with the Glenstal Abbey monks.

In 2000, I was invited to join the board of advisors, the only monastic outsider, working on *The Glenstal Book of Prayer*. Produced by the only male Benedictine monastery in Ireland, this book was, as you would expect, centred on the Roman Catholic tradition and the monastic daily round. It became an immediate bestseller and continues to be popular.

I acted as a midwife to the book; its eventual gift to me was as a stimulus to a further exploration of prayer and its sister, ritual. By this time, my sons were in third-level education, I had separated from their father and begun a doctorate in Theology (which I received in 2003) and was living at the time on the grounds of Glenstal Abbey. Every day, I abided by the monks' daily routine of liturgical prayer. Observing this community, albeit from afar, I learned more than I have as yet been able to assimilate about how to pray in a ritualistic manner.

Gradually, I craved a more inclusive approach to devotion. This was something of a revelation to me as, up to then, I'd always been more than comfortable with my own Christian devotions and prayer space. At the time, the yearning towards ministry haunted me constantly. The Cuban–Spanish author, Anaïs Nin, articulates such a moment of transition in life, often too easy to miss or too daunting to face up to: I held my fire *'until the day came when the risk to remain tight in a bud was more painful than the risk it took to blossom'*.

A greater desire to know, and to live out, ritual prayers from other religious traditions welled up inside me. Not only this, but I yearned to share them with others. But how was I to follow this gigantic change of life? How could I possibly pursue a life of ministry, which was completely out of the question for any woman in my own tradition? Long story short, a friend introduced me to the OneSpirit Interfaith Foundation Seminary in London. I was off. I left my little monastery garden hermitage and, in July 2017, I was ordained an Interfaith minister. One of the greatest grace-filled moments of my life.

Of course, my Christian heritage will always be the most familiar and comfortable to me, yet I am enthralled by other faith perspectives. In this book, I want to share all of these with you, in the hope that you too will be nourished by them. There are treasures – and indeed dark crevices – in all faiths but whatever your nudgings of the holy are, every religion has universal teachings. In my own faith journey, I see this a kind of spiritual cross-fertilisation where truths from various traditions combine and fuse to create an authentic expression of love and personal growth. In other words, the many freshwater streams eventually meet at the estuary to the ocean of eternity.

Throughout this treasury, I have presented my long-time belief that all of life, every experience, is a kneeling bench

– a *prie-dieu* – for prayer. To employ another word, life is a sacrament that, as we learned from our catechisms, is an outward sign of divine grace or presence. It seems to me that many people believe sacraments are confined too narrowly to certain organisational 'Church' occasions and events, whereas, in reality, they are much more pervasive and ubiquitous.

Sacraments can neither be limited nor quantified. They are anywhere and everywhere – a rabbit in a field at evening time, a peregrine soaring through the air, the smile of a friend, the plight of that same friend in need; these are all sacraments sent to remind us of the presence of another dimension of life. An invisible world made manifest in the visible. *Theosony*, to use a neologism for the existence of God through sound, describes the sacramental litany of sound that surrounds us day and night. In the Christian tradition, the Gospel of John (3:8) narrates Jesus defining the Holy Spirit as aural – you *'hear the sound of it'*.

Our entire life is a sacrament if we can but hear and see the Divine beyond the threshold of human aural and visual perception.

This book is a treatise of my lifelong, sometimes stammering, conversation with the realm of a higher Other. I am sharing as intimately and as honestly as I am able, however, my motivation is not egotistical or narcissistic.

This is your story too. The Divine uniquely lives in you and, through sharing my story, it becomes a part of yours. '*Mo scéal féin, scéal gach duine*' is an ageless Irish proverb. It proposes that your personal parable resonates with mine and with everyone else's.

A prayer ritual is my homecoming, a place of refuge and retreat. I can relax into it and really be. The inner walls of a sacred prayer, poem, blessing or ritual is layered with the souls, the spirits, the presence of those who have gone before. In Ireland, we live in two worlds; the visible and the invisible Otherworld where a host of 'daoine maithe' – good ancestors dwell. Enter the world of ritual and you are on the threshold between both.

In this book, I draw on wisdom from many sacred texts and reveal some of my private, subjective expressions of prayer. Although you will encounter some inter-religious invocations, the main focus will be the two traditions that have fed my heart – the Celtic, Irish tradition on the one hand, and the Christian practice in which I was raised on the other. However, welcoming into my life the treasures of other faiths has enriched enormously my dedication, appreciation and allegiance to Christ's message of faith, hope and love.

All the rituals and prayer-poems given in this book have

evolved into my practice over the years. Every single one has moved me in some way and at some moment in my life. The premise is that if these prayers and rituals are witness to the Divine for me, they will enhance the spiritual, inner life of all into whose hands this book of rituals comes.

For me, poetry is an avenue to the Divine and I do not make any distinction between a poem and a prayer. In the Irish language, the connection is specific. A prayer is *Dán Dé* – a poem of God. Poets open our eyes and ears to see and hear that which we has long forgotten. Poetry can cure contemplative amnesia. The Celestial is waiting in ambush to leap out from a line, a stanza or even one word. The authentic spiritual insight within sacred rituals is within reach of every person, young and old; to be human is to experience the entire plethora of emotions, doubts, fears and ecstasy.

For some years now, I have been teaching a module on Ritual and Liturgy at Mary Immaculate College, University of Limerick. As I get to know my students and they me, I begin by inviting a student to join me at the top of the classroom – if possible, this student is a tall, bearded, spectacle-wearing, hoodie-sporting young man. I invite the other students to name the many dissimilarities between us. Then, turning to the student, I ask if he has ever felt. 'Have you ever felt happy? Did you ever cry? Have you laughed in your life? Have you ever despaired?' The shy response will always be in the positive; the students have always felt these emotions. I may sometimes, intuiting the nature of the student, add the question: 'Have you ever prayed?', trusting that the response will be affirmative. 'So what is the moral here?' I ask. It is that deep things are common to us all. So too is our universal primeval quest for ritual and prayer. Prayer can help us to move through life with our emotions – to reflect on them and to sit with them, and sometimes to ask for comfort. Every one of us experiences the need for connection, and a relationship to a higher power is the deepest form of connection of all. This book will help you on your journey to establishing a sacred space for prayer in your life, giving you the tools and confidence you need to welcome ritual into your everyday.

CAD ATÁ I GCEIST AGAM :
What do the terms ritual, prayer and blessing mean to me?

In my experience, all three terms – 'ritual', 'prayer', 'blessing' – are synonymous. They all outline a trinity of sources to a homecoming, a sanctuary of daily refuge and retreat – 'the key of the morning and the bolt of the evening', as Mahatma Gandhi put it.

This trilogy wakens and invigorates the heart and soul in the morning and tucks it into bed at night. Psalm 5 says: *'O Lord, in the morning you hear my voice; in the morning, I plead my case to you.'* Psalm 4 reminds us, *'I lie down in peace and sleep comes at once, for you alone make me dwell in safety.'* No sleeping tablets, melatonin or tranquilisers are needed, and no side-effects save a sound sleep and wholesome dreams. Padre Pio, a twentieth-century friar and saint in the Catholic tradition, believed that the air we inhale is simply prayer – 'the oxygen of the soul'.

So, a ritual, prayer and blessing form a three-way conversation between equals, between comrades.

A ritual always functions on subtle suggestion, not precise descriptions, inviting us to see new horizons, richness and mystery as it unfurls. Description is often the proprietor of sameness and tedium, but prayer, ritual and blessing call upon our imaginations to bind us to ourselves, to others and to the Higher Source in unforeseen possibilities. An encounter with this trio always leaves the final step towards wholeness up to you and your own happenstance with it. However, nothing in the realm of prayer is perfect because not only is nothing in life flawless but the perfect would be so uninteresting and bland.

Prayer through ritual is where the human heart meets the Divine heart.

We all have rituals in our daily lives – the morning cup of coffee, the shower, cooking, charging the phone – the things we carry out almost mindlessly. But, looking at a routine consciously activates a higher appliance of ritual. So many people label their identity with a higher force as 'spiritual' rather than religious that it's now a cliché. But play around with the word, break it apart and you get spi-ritual – ritual is spirit, a secret force circling our lives. It is our turning to the God of our familiar understanding, letting that presence enter, that transforms our ordinary lives. As St Francis held: 'Prayer is the answer to life … Prayer moistens the heart and the earth'.

Ritual is a fact of life. In its simplest form, it is an awakening of new blessing in and through its expression. Every human society revolves around rites of passage. Even shaking hands or sharing a greeting is a gift. Life is ritual and while it may be familiar, its source is the transparency, the clarity, of the unexpected and the tantalising. There are no descriptions, no recipes, no instructions, a ritual is merely a suggestion. It is only hinted at. When ritual becomes verbose and rational, the threshold between the inner and outer self collapses. We have witnessed this over and over again, framed within the tired rituals of institutionalism. And these tired rituals can often attract more attention to the performance of the ritual rather than the meaning. A ritual that is haphazard and excludes anyone remains a fossilised, sterile exercise.

During my first visit to India in 1982, I learned that prayer and ritual are etched into the day there. Turn a corner in any busy city street and there is a Hindu shrine to a deity where *puja* (gifts to the gods) are offered. Amid the amazing chaos, God is everywhere. Look at the name 'India' (derived originally from the river Sindhu) through an Irish lens and you see IN-DIA meaning 'in God'. The Celtic psyche agrees, firstly, on this *Dia uile-laithreach* (God ever present and everywhere in all creation without being identified with any of it). I have visited India, a place I now think of as another home, many times, each one an eye – or rather an ear – opener into the great sacrament of daily prayer blessing.

Another similarity between Ireland and India is the way people greet one another. Indian divine recognition is also beautifully realised in body prayer along with verbal greeting. Hands are joined palm to palm and head bowed to bless the presence of the other with the trisyllabic salutation 'Namaste', or Namasgar, originally a salutation for the gods and now often translated as '*the Divine in me bows to the Divine in you*'. The Irish version is '*Go mbeannaí Dia dhuit*' – May God bless you. God is part of simple everyday moments of life – right down to the way we say hello to each other. During that first visit to India, I also learned of the Chakras. Originating from the ancient Indian Sanskrit scriptures, the Vedas, a chakra means a circle, a point or a wheel, and the seven circles of spiritual energy are wedded to seven centres of the human body. I was immediately struck by the intimacy in sound between Sanskrit and the Irish language. To translate 'seven wheels' into Irish, is 'seacht roth' which sounds exactly like chak-ra. These seven circles of body energy are now woven into my daily ritual practice, which I will share with you later.

In Hindu and Buddhist practice, a guru is essential to your existence and is someone who accompanies and teaches you along the spiritual path. A *theosonic* (God-sounding) root word in Sansrit, 'guru' comes from *gu* (ignorance/darkness) and *ru* (dismisser of darkness), a guru is anyone (or anything), that banishes or balances the gloomy shadows of our thinking/lives. There is, of course, the guru within ourselves – and ritual is where these two streams merge and combine to create the one river of expression, which is the spirit and ritual – The Spiritual.

Ritual is the objectification that recognises you as both another human being and as a spirit-filled possibility. An American friend of mine is fond of saying that we are our own gurus because if read aloud letter by letter it sounds like: *Gee, You are You*. Rather trite but there's a smidgeon of truth to it too. Ritual is a powerful key that unlocks the door to self-knowledge, inner joy and the rich diversity that dwells within you. The intention of this treasury is to explore and experience this together. What is so exciting, so liberating, is that there is no single time or way for these complex depths to surface. Prayer and ritual teach us new truths about ourselves and we become more grounded on the one hand, yet united with Divine imagination on the other. Prayer and ritual hold the key to the ultimate mystery of where we have come from, what it is that keeps us going and where our final destination will be.

Prayer and ritual are the essence of all religions. An experience of ceremony can lighten the heavy weight of a troubled and troubling life. Ritualistic awareness is the gateway to our own soul. The minutiae of life are occasions of ritual and no one who has been gifted with human presence is denied the beauty and inner sanctuary of ritual. Prayer, whether spoken aloud, read quietly or simply dwelling in silence is the core expression of ritual; the permanent resident in this tabernacle, this Holy of Holies of the human heart.

All rituals are rich prayer sources that can transform human society. It is through a shared belief and practice in this communal world of prayer that our cosmic beginnings will be guided and directed. However, we must liberate ourselves from old, redundant paradigms of prayer. So many people carry second-hand thoughts about prayerful ritual; inherited notions, where praying is somewhere outside of them, outdated and institutional, wedged between novena and pilgrimage, ashram and sangha, mindfulness and contemplation. Nothing could be further from the truth.

Anything you do, from the first light of morning to the depths of night's darkness, can be an act of discovery, another definition of prayer. Spoken, sung, whispered or silent – the praying space is entirely your choice. Stand, sit, lie down, walk or dance as you go. Let this precious sacred means of finding belonging to ourselves not be diminished or misunderstood as sentimental, piteous, harsh or inflexible.

The manual section of this book is my own Do It Yourself guide, leading to the greatest treasure we possess – the creation and living out of our own ritualistic journey. Every prayer and rite in this book is testimony to what I want to say to you about awakening your heart to your mystical depths. My hope and prayer for you is that whenever you pick up this little book, you will be nudged into discovering the secret dimension of prayer within yourself that guarantees you wholeness and happiness.

CUMHACHT NA PAIDREOIREACHTA:
The Power of Ritual

R itual and blessing are expressions of pure prayer where we commend our deepest moments of longing to a supreme force. In so doing, we let go and surrender our struggles and trials and, of course, our elations. We honour our ancestors and the angelic beings, we attend to heart matters with the love poems of others and ourselves – from life after painful friendships, from blessings in times of destitution to embracing inevitable ageing, dying and death. The glory of the Divine glows in these expressions.

Just as we gather together the ingredients of a meal before we start to cook, so we should prepare ourselves and our praying space before we move towards the Divine.

However, as I've already said, we can welcome and 'do' prayer at any time, in any space and without any 'ingredients'. Do not think that this beautiful act requires a physical sacred platform – be moved to pray as you travel. A journey becomes sacred when you pray! As Rabia of Basra, the eighth-century female Muslim saint and Sufi mystic, put it: *'Prayer should bring us to an altar where no walls or names exist.'*

Yet, by carefully and purposefully setting up your individual, personal praying space, you are taking the first step towards hallowing the duration of your own ceremonial timeout. I will guide you through this later with simple ideas that will inspire you to add your own signature.

Rituals and blessings and prayers are soul triplets that leave us radically changed in the doing. It is the spirit that is a secret force circling our lives. Julian of Norwich, the first known female writer in the English language, knew of this life-giving potency: *'Prayer is not an idle occupation. It's a very powerful instrument of our work and love'.*

The embodiment of prayer is to understand all of this and is the most wholesome medicine to ease the longing and pain of the broken-hearted. Through my own practices, I realised that the original restorative templates of prayers have failed miserably in the past to provide safe and secure shelter for our refugee souls. These institutional ritualistic paradigms, such as liturgy and the sacraments, all lacked imagination, creativity, personal introspection and the power of blessings. A new, richer and deeper contemporary landscape of personal prayer and ritual is at the centre of a more mystical, contemplative way of being – and is the intention of this treasury.

We are freeing the clogged channels of spirit within ourselves and making our own vibrant temples for prayer and ritual.

For too long, the word 'prayer' has resonated with people as a weary, outworn notion of how we talk to God. More and more, we are being inundated with secularism and relentless images of doom and gloom in these challenging days. Attention to the power of ritual, not to mention prayer, is often scoffed at as being churchy, romantic and silly. Yet, the passion and the life of prayer is deeply insulated and shielded within every soul. The Spirit thrives on the awakening and flowering of the discovery of the blueprint of the divine.

The soul is the breastplate, the protector of our innermost longing. Take the pencil with which I am writing these initial notes. The charcoal lead is the soul, carefully protected by the wooden casing – the armour around it – the outer appearance to the world. This pencil is worthless without a driving force to guide it, which is the Spirit, waiting patiently for a human hand to interpret the message.

The radical truth is that our prayer life has nothing to do with facts or status, age, situation or power. It is all about how to be alive in a culture preoccupied with busyness and deaf to mystery. Attention to prayer, as noticing or responding to our own pencil intuitions is a profound mining of self-worth and love. In short, prayer is a conversàtion with your inner self about your place in the world and with the Divine.

Below is an inventory of soul questions that will help you to start your journey of authentic self-discovery. Take your pencil and record your own answers in your journal or in the Notaí pages at the end of this book. Stamp each entry with the date because you may return to it at a future time and your answers may evolve over time.

- Do you wonder why you're here and what your purpose is?

- Have you lost sight of what matters most in your life?

- Do you feel lonely and crave real belonging, friendship and togetherness?

- Have you ever doubted or queried the existence of a higher power, a guiding force?

- Do you envy mystics and holy people?

If you answered yes to any of these, know that you're not alone. These uncertainties send our souls off-course without a navigational chart. Ambiguity, self-criticism, fear and doubt can drown out the wonder of our own being.

The manual that follows will help you, as it does for me, to discern and create a sacred space in the midst of all the pain, fears and doubts that engulf us. In turn and time, two worlds live in harmony in a dualism that is harmonious and transforming. The inevitable realm of our flawed, weak nature is not only welcomed into the space of ritual and prayer but, in so doing, our frailties actually deepen our capacity for love of ourselves and one another.

KAIROS NAOFA : Making Time for Yourself Every Day

What was the chronology of your day yesterday? You rose in the morning, and the hours began their unrelenting toll on your life. The chronological clock ticked loudly, often bullying us into apathy and stupor. Taking time out in the day is always a moveable, ever-changing feast in life. Careers, relationships, family rearing, retirement, illness, anxiety, and so on, all determine our daylight and night-time chronometry. (Incidentally, I love that honeyed sound of 'chronometry'. Say it aloud, see or hear it for yourself. The term is birthed out of a Greek word *chronos,* which is best understood by its English sister 'chronology'.)

Our little lives are detailed timetables of the rituals we carry out, morning, noon and night.

Ancient Greece honoured another time space that was a precious timeout to be with our inner selves: *prayer* time. This they named *kairos.* In India, there was a similar distinction between ordinary and extraordinary time. *Kala* is the Sanskrit concept of *chronos* and *ritu,* like *kairos* is spiritual time.

A ritual is all time elevated to a new dimension, offered up as it were to a higher source. Early Greek translations of the Bible refer to time as *kairos,* an opportune period for renewal and self-discovery, and to feel God's grace. How much more precious and wonderful does the familiar passage from Ecclesiastes become when we pray: *'To everything there is a kairos for every matter under heaven: a kairos to be born and a kairos to die … a kairos to be silent and a kairos to speak.'* This habit of seeing time as precious transformation is a ritual in itself.

Kairos is surely what the twelfth-century mystic, Benedictine Abbess and visionary, called '*viriditas*' or greening, the life-force energy of inner and outer identity. '*In God's own time*' is the Irish imagination's spelling out of the good of it. This is a mantra that I call on when I leave myself, as my mother used to say at the end of a demanding day, with no time even to bless myself!

No one knows who wrote ten-fold advice given below but it does exalt the concept of setting aside that *kairos* daily. In harmony with the theme of this book, our one sacred duty is find and know prayer-time.

❋❋❋❋❋❋❋❋❋❋❋❋❋❋❋❋❋❋❋❋❋

Take time to think; it is the source of power.
Take time to read; it is the foundation of wisdom.
Take time to play; it is the secret of staying young.
Take time to be quiet; it is the opportunity to seek God.
Take time to be aware; it is the opportunity to help others.
Take time to love and be loved; it is God's greatest gift.
Take time to laugh; it is the music of the soul.
Take time to be friendly; it is the road to happiness.
Take time to dream; it is what the future is made of.
Take time to pray; it is the greatest power on earth.
Anonymous

❋❋❋❋❋❋❋❋❋❋❋❋❋❋❋❋❋❋❋❋❋

NA SEACHT TREOIREACHA :
The ritual of the seven directions

There was a monastic movement in early Ireland called the Céilí Dé (servants of God). The first written records of their presence dates to the eighth century. From these records, we have lovely testimonies of how our forefathers prayed daily with complete attention whilst turning towards six directions – the east, west, north, south, the sky above and the earth below. As you read this treasury, remember that you are a part-time modern-day member of the Céilí Dé.

Similarly, the Vedas, the oldest scriptures of Hinduism (and perhaps the oldest scriptures in the world), contain a volume of poetry known as 'The Rig Veda'. This volume also presents a blessing in the five cardinal directions – north, south, east, west and here. So, where your heart is, there is your home, as Christian Scriptures would say.

Add to this, a Native American prayer that I gathered along the way when I was a visiting scholar in Berkeley, California, in 2003, and the circle of the global sacredness of direction is complete – from our ancestors in India, to Ireland to America.

As we prepare to develop our own prayer ritual space and routine, let us first go through this early ritual as an example of what we can achieve.

❋✳❋✳❋✳❋✳❋✳❋✳❋✳❋✳❋✳❋✳❋✳❋✳❋

Firstly, light a candle. If you remain seated during this, simply turn your head towards each direction. If you stand, move your body to face the direction. I like to raise my hands to greet each direction while I pray. As you move to the next cardinal station, lower your hands to your side ready to lift them up again at the next turning.

❋✳❋✳❋✳❋✳❋✳❋✳❋✳❋✳❋✳❋✳❋✳❋✳❋

Opening Prayer

I gather this morning as did my ancestors of old with our deep joys, griefs, gifts and various needs. Let us call on the Great Spirit to acknowledge and cross into a new threshold that this day holds.

*Grandfather, Great Spirit, once more behold me on earth
and lean to hear my feeble voice. You lived first, and you are
older than all need, older than all prayer. All things belong
to you – the two-leggeds, the four-leggeds, the wings of the air
and all green things that live. You have set the powers of the
four quarters to cross each other. The good road and the road
of difficulties you have made to cross; and where they cross,
the place is holy [PLACE OF RITUAL]. Day in and day out,
forever, you are the life of things. Therefore, I am sending a voice,
Great Spirit, my grandfather, forgetting nothing you have made,
the stars of the universe and the grasses of the earth.*
Black Elk Oglala, Sioux

AN OIRTHEAR : The East

Turning eastwards represented the saving presence of God. According to holy texts, on the Day of Judgment, God/Allah will appear from the east. Turning towards this Divine source first and foremost, sanctifies the blessing ritual to follow. The entrance to the Garden of Eden faced east (Gen 2:8) and churches are oriented toward the east because it is the locus of Jerusalem and the Holy Land.

The east – the Latin *oriens* meaning 'to rise' – is where the sun ascends, and so this is the direction of new beginnings, hope, promise and potential. Prosperity and farming identify eastwards. Green, the colour of the earth and growth, represents the east. So, look now, and bless the earth under your feet.

I always call on Hildegard von Bingen, the twelfth-century Benedictine Abbess, as I pray to this eastern course for two reasons. The peacock feather at my altar reminds me too that I – and you – along with her are a 'feather on the breath of God'. Secondly, her wild and fiery relationship with the Divine was always 'viriditas' – greening, thriving and prosperous.

❋·❋·❋·❋·❋·❋·❋·❋·❋·❋·❋·❋·❋·❋·❋·❋·❋·❋

Let us pray
A Spiorad anoir (O Spirit of the East)
'In the morning, fill us with your love.' (Psalm 90)
Yours is the morning, O bright East, the invisible air and the spring. I pray that I may be open to receiving the newness of life, greening of spirit and cleansing of heart this day. Stay with me in times of fresh beginnings and eras of sowing new seeds.

❋·❋·❋·❋·❋·❋·❋·❋·❋·❋·❋·❋·❋·❋·❋·❋·❋·❋

AN DEISCEART: The South

Now move a quarter turn to your right to face the south – you are turning and travelling in harmony. The term 'south' is derived from the Old English word meaning 'sun' from the fact that it is the direction of the sun at noon in the northern hemisphere, the right-hand side of the rising sun. It is the direction of warmth, growth, fertility, creativity and productivity. It is the midwife of music and poetry.

In addition, this direction represents hope, trust and faithfulness in relationships. On the Incan Medicine Wheel, the south is where you engage with your past. The archetype here is the serpent that sheds its skin for survival and future. Passionate, vivid and intense, red is the south's hue – the colour of blood and belonging, the onset of womanhood. The south urges us to celebrate wildly.

Begin your prayer to the south by focusing on your candle, the symbol of southern fire, which removes the dross from our lives and moulds us into a new creation.

❈⟡❈⟡❈⟡❈⟡❈⟡❈⟡❈⟡❈⟡❈⟡❈⟡❈⟡❈⟡❈⟡❈

Let us pray
A Spioraid aneas (O Spirit of the South)
'And by God's power, he led out the South wind.' (Psalm 78:26)

Stay with us through the heat of the day and help us to do our work as you wish for us. We thank you for the gift of poetry, music and imagination. Help us to rid ourselves – to burn from our hearts – all that haunts us at this moment. Teach us how to celebrate your presence and your offerings.

❋⁜❋⁜❋⁜❋⁜❋⁜❋⁜❋⁜❋⁜❋⁜❋⁜❋⁜❋⁜❋⁜❋

AN tIARTHAR : The West

Turn to the right and face west. The West – in Latin *occidens,* meaning 'to fall away' – is the path the sun follows as it sinks to rest. Dream-catching, dreaming thrives here. Evening and autumn are its incarnation. When the soul is on its final journey and preparing for the oncoming adventure of resurrection, it is in the west that it rests a while. The west is the seat of learning, Sophia, wisdom and knowledge. Black is the colour when the sun sinks into darkness.

❋⁜❋⁜❋⁜❋⁜❋⁜❋⁜❋⁜❋⁜❋⁜❋⁜❋⁜❋⁜❋⁜❋

Let us pray
A Spioraid aniar (O Spirit of the West)
'From the rising of the sun unto its setting, praise be the name of the Lord.' (Psalm 113:3)

I offer my dreams to you, both night-time reveries and daytime longings. May I have the discernment and the ears to hear what whisperings and nudges I can really trust and need to follow.

May you, O West, the autumnal direction where everything dies and prepares for the new life of resurrection fill me with courage and hope in the face of death. Teach us to let go of life when the final call comes peacefully and with ease as the sun goes down.

❋＊❋＊❋＊❋＊❋＊❋＊❋＊❋＊❋＊❋＊❋＊❋＊❋

AN TUAISCEART: The North

The North – related to an Old High German word *ner* meaning 'left' – as it is to the left of the rising sun. It is the direction of the cold, of winds, of strength, courage, fortitude, might, single-mindedness, focus, clarity and purpose. The winterland of the north is the place of hibernation. 'Out of the North comes the golden splendour of God,' Job proclaimed (Job 37:22).

This is the ancient direction and its colour – red – reflects that antiquity from which everything emerged and emerges. Here resides darkness, mystery and magic.

The spirit of mountains, bogs, lakes and seas is embodied here, and we must move around this direction to understand shape and form. Yet we must keep our distance to treasure its vastness. Then we draw near to the life of the north.

Now as you turn, feel the ground beneath your feet. The earth is the element symbolising the North. In Native American traditions, this direction holds out trials and the purification of ourselves to endure these hardships.

✺⁂✺⁂✺⁂✺⁂✺⁂✺⁂✺⁂✺⁂✺⁂✺⁂✺⁂✺⁂✺

Let us pray
A Spioraid aduaidh (O Spirit of the North)

'I lift up my eyes to the mountains, from where shall come my help.' (Psalm 120)

Shelter me under your wings as I hibernate in the winterland of my heart, O North. Like the snowdrop in spring, nourish my inner roots to survive the sanctuary of darkness, lift my little head above the snows to herald life and joy for myself and others. Help me in my hardships and troubles that at times overwhelm me.

✺⁂✺⁂✺⁂✺⁂✺⁂✺⁂✺⁂✺⁂✺⁂✺⁂✺⁂✺⁂✺

AN SPÉIR : The Sky
Turn back to the east, you have come full circle. Now, look above you to the sky, a place that, for Native Americans and the Celts, is the home of Father Sky.

The sun, moon, clouds and stars are ingenious features of our planet that we overlook or are unable to picture. Viewed as a metaphor for the spiritual, the immensity of the sky is rich in meaning. Although the clouds may darken it, day or night, there is still the blue sky and the shining sun above or the twinkling galaxy in the darkness. *Súil Dé* – the eye of God – is our sun. In the Scottish Hebrides, the humble, reverential gesture was to uncover your head and bow at the sight of the sun in the sky.

✺❀✺❀✺❀✺❀✺❀✺❀✺❀✺❀✺❀✺❀✺❀✺❀✺❀✺❀✺

Let us pray
A Spioraid an spéir, an gealach, an ghriain agus na réaltaí
(O Spirit of the sky, the moon, the sun and the stars)

'The Heavens are telling the glory of God and the firmament proclaims God's handiwork.' (Psalm 19:1)

O grandfather Sky, you look down upon us, animating our actions and our lives. We pray to you for clarity and strength for the ears to hear our hearts' inner desires, to shift our tired patterns of life and bring us safely into the new realm of change and challenge.

O brother Sun: Your rays reflect the light of my self-realisation and growth, where I can truly find my best self. May the radiance of the rising sun, ignite my vital spark of courage and boldness and let that fire cleanse and purify our hearts and souls. O sister Moon: Help me to respect my emotions, instincts and divine feminine energy, feeling more sensitive or nurturing to others.

We pray that our minds, souls and spirits will not forget to look upward this day, to the One who is so much greater than we are. We give thanks for your rich rays as you gently traverse the sky; teach us how to tread the path of life with that same gentleness, patience and reverence.

✺✲✺✲✺✲✺✲✺✲✺✲✺✲✺✲✺✲✺✲✺✲✺✲✺✲✺✲✺

AN DOMHAIN: The earth

Now, kneel where you are, if this is comfortable for you. Place your palms firmly on the earth and bow low. Humanity has much to apologise for. To our own appalling peril, we have inflicted intolerable pain and cruelty on earth's home, hearth and heart. The Covid wake-up call for us all has been around connection and awareness of the beauty of our environment on the one hand, and grief and sadness at the plundering, the senselessness, the greed that human tragic drama that we have all played our roles in on the other.

May this ritual today be our evolutionary step into owning our responsibility now. We have over eight billion neighbours on this planet but fifty per cent of them are hungry, thirsty and dying before our eyes, and we need to do something about it. Two thirds of our family is without water and living through drought.

❋⚹❋⚹❋⚹❋⚹❋⚹❋⚹❋⚹❋⚹❋⚹❋⚹❋⚹❋⚹❋⚹❋

Let us pray

A Spioraid an Talamh mhór (O Spirit of the great earth)
'The earth is the Lord's and all that's in it.' (Psalm 24:1)

Maith dhúinn ár bpeacaí: Forgive us our trespasses, O Mother Earth. We are so sorry for pain we have caused you when we refused to listen to your cries.

Help us to dwell in your house with respect now, to radically redress the balance of treating you well. May everything I do this day be in honour and reverence of you, Mother Earth. In so doing, may I take my place, humbly and remorsefully, in the queue of history, between my ancestors and my children yet to come.

We pray for an altered attitude towards consumerism, global warming, water pollution, disastrous and greedy economic growth, racism, genderism and a transmuted environment that will gently enable our self-indulgence, our gluttony, to collapse and die.

Today, I pledge to transform my consciousness to one of mutual, collective awareness. May I undertake through my cosmic prayer to share what I do not need. Let me take stock and appreciate what I have and give thanks.

❈✻❈✻❈✻❈✻❈✻❈✻❈✻❈✻❈✻❈✻❈✻❈✻❈

AN CROÍ : The Heart

Rise now and place your hands on your heart, in the centre of your chest – the final cardinal direction of existence. Here is your prayer nerve-centre where the Spirit resides. Journeying into the inner heart is the panacea for all ills. *'Where your treasure is, there your heart is also.'* (Matt 6:21) So now in obedience to Rainer Maria Rilke, 'work of the eyes is done, now go and do the heart work … on all the images imprisoned within you'.

❈✻❈✻❈✻❈✻❈✻❈✻❈✻❈✻❈✻❈✻❈✻❈✻❈

Let us pray

A Spioraid mo chroí agus m'anam (O Spirit of my heart and soul)

'My heart is steadfast, O God, my heart is steadfast. I will sing and make music, Awake my soul.' (Psalm 57:7–8)

Spirit of my heart, bring me your peace today in the silence of compassion. Liberate me to be fully alive to myself, to others and to you. From your depths, give me the courage to persist and live without fear and turmoil. Help me carry the load of my own frequent heavy lonesome heart.

And finally, we bring you all our prayers to the bright light of this morning. May we walk justly today where air is pure, where earth is green and greening, in harmony with the sun and the moon, with the ebb and flow of mother ocean, in the tranquillity of our hearts and most of all in the intimacy of human and blessed conversation and belonging.

❊❊❊❊❊❊❊❊❊❊❊❊❊❊❊❊❊❊❊❊❊

Now, that we have shared a ritual of blessing for the directions, let us leave the *focail scoir* – the final word – to the prophet Jeremiah: '*Stand at the crossroads, and look, and ask for the ancient paths, where the good way lies and walk in it and find rest for your souls*'. (Jeremiah 6:16)

AN LÁMHLEABHAR :
The Manual

How can *you* enter this new way of prayer and ritual that has been waiting for you all these years?

Here, dear reader, is where we build your own bridge that will transport you to your own path to ritual, prayer and blessing. It's more of a drawbridge really that, when lowered, will carry you to Divine safety and, when raised, will protect your inner world from outer distraction and malevolence.

TÚS MAITH LEATH NA HOIBRE :
A Good Beginning Is Half the Work (Irish proverb)

Most faiths agree that, before we begin any new work, we should bless our intention and commend it to a Higher Source, whether it be the Divine, the Almighty, the Holy

Blessed One, Allah, Waheguru, Shiva, the Deity, Brahman, Yahweh and Buddha. This preparatory offering, as in all the other rituals to follow, can be adapted to whatever belief system that is home for you.

St Benedict advises in the introduction to *The Rule*: '*First of all, with instant prayer, beg that God would bring to completion every good you set out to do*'.

So let us open ourselves up to the surprise and wonder that is the fundamental nature of prayer. Create a quiet moment – a short one-minute pause. Be aware of the tasks ahead of you.

DO THEARMAINN URNAÍ:
Your Prayer Sanctuary

☼❊☼❊☼❊☼❊☼❊☼❊☼❊☼❊☼❊☼❊☼❊☼❊☼❊☼

'But whenever you pray, go into your room and shut the door and pray to your Father who is in secret, and your Father who sees in secret will reward you.'
(Matthew 6:6)

☼❊☼❊☼❊☼❊☼❊☼❊☼❊☼❊☼❊☼❊☼❊☼❊☼❊☼

This is one of my favourite passages from Scripture, but it is only one half of the equation. The Gospel of Mark (6:31) completes the prayer picture: *'Come away by yourself … and refresh yourselves for a little'*. Chapter six in both gospels encourages us 'chillax', as the American portmanteau defines it. I invite you to enter into your prayer space, that special place where you can hear and speak with God.

The Irish language names a church as *Teach Dé* – the house, the home of God. There is an intimacy about this that means that this is your hearth space. We come into this holy dwelling with the same reverence that we enter our own family homes where our troubled minds are set at peace and where the weight of the world immediately slips from our shoulders. This is what every prayer under the sun is about. It harbours a gathered memory of humanity, a living, breathing archive of godliness, a sanctuary of Absolute Presence.

So let us take the first step in our prayer pilgrimage with a poem.

As we prepare to take pragmatic steps into constructing our own prayer space, here is a poem by my son, Mícheál. It describes a moment with his Hindu mother-in-law, Maya, in her prayer room during a visit to her home a few years ago.

This is my prayer room
No one comes in.
I anoint icons here
with sandalwood and pour
milk over deity's chanting
a throaty mantra.
I sat cross-legged
till I could no more.
But don't worry,
my god already knows
my aches and pains.
This altar holds my trinkets
of faith, the tools of prayer,
instruments of hope, and
rag offerings to my elephant god.
If you wish to pray, I'll let you,
turning halfway through
my rosary making sure
you're comfortable.
Tuesday's prayers are slightly longer,
you see.
The incense will rise for you and I,
for there is peace in worship
at the foot of a virgin mother

and a blue-skinned baby.
The gurus and martyrs,
the saints and angels.

And when I hand you the bell, ring it.
Not once, but keep ringing
till I tell you. Pray with me.
Say the words, ring the bell
We're almost there.
This part is my favourite,
It's where God feels the closest.
So ask for mercy or for help
or forgiveness, no need to tell.
For my story is your story,
is everybody's story.

Let the bell stop ringing now.
We've prayed well today,
thank you for your silence
I know my god is pleased
to meet you, sees your sad
eyes and sweet spirit
and knows you
have much more to do.

'This Is My Prayer Room', Mícheál Ó Súilleabháin

❋❖❋❖❋❖❋❖❋❖❋❖❋❖❋❖❋❖❋❖❋❖❋❖❋❖❋

The Altar

What is an altar?

Originally, the word meant a '*high space*' (from the Latin *altus*). In Judaism, it implied a place of sacrifice, and Christianity blended both meanings. In church buildings, the altar faces east and is usually elevated by steps; it is a no-go area for everyone except the male clergy. In contrast, an altar in our homes is a space of intimate belonging, a sanctuary.

In Eastern Orthodoxy, every home is a temple, the heart of which is the Icon (Red) Corner that also faces east.

An altar is simply an aperitif to prayer, a space that reminds us to offer our prayers. A word here on an altar on the move before I outline my own home high space. We can carry an altar in our hearts as well as in our suitcases. When I travel, before I even unpack my luggage, I choose a prayer corner in my temporary room – normally on the dressing table – and set up a travelling altar. First out of my little canvas roaming altar bag is the nightlight and matches, which I set before the mirror to amplify the flame light. Then a miniature square Russian nineteenth-century icon of Mary that a monastic friend gifted to me years ago. A little vial of holy water, my Psalm book and a notebook with some prayer poems, a bell, and that's it. Usually, the dressing table is away from a window where I will not be distracted and can really focus on my prayer. Then I know that, from this little makeshift sacred site, I can challenge any thorny worries that my soul may have to encounter in the days ahead.

'*In my soul, there is a temple, a shrine, a mosque, a church that dissolve, that dissolve in God,*' as Rabia of Basra, the eighth-century female Islamic saint and Sufi mystic, claimed.

D'ALTÓIR FHÉINIG: Creating Your Altar

No two people, no two altars, will be the same. What follows are just some guidelines to get you motivated to create your unique high space.

AN CHOINEALL BEO: The Living Candle

The first thing we need to create our altar is your favourite candle. This forms a centrepiece and a focus not only for all the other 'ingredients' that you include, but for your gaze in moments of silence and contemplation. Position this candle on some piece of colourful fabric, according to the natural or liturgical seasons. A little pragmatic tip here: spread out the cloth flat on the ground. Then put your candle at the centre. Rotate the candle on the cloth and, miraculously, an artistic spiral will form before your eyes!

Almost all of our rituals, those of both celebration and sadness, include the lighting of a candle. It seems that as long as the candle burns, all will be well. So many of our rituals would be dull without them: the blowing out of the birthday cake candles, Christmas candles in the windows, dining-table candles to grace a meal, lantern candles at the door to greet guests and strangers. In Ireland, a request for prayer will often be: '*Will you light a candle for me?*' This entreaty now limps on one wing having entirely lost its second half – '*when you go to church*'.

The most popular ritual sought after and considered essential in the wedding ceremonies I officiate is the lighting of the Unity Candle. I also suggest another lighting ritual, since a marriage is not simply celebrating the two lovers before our eyes, it is also joining of two families. Why not have a family unity candle too? So, at the beginning of the ceremony after I welcome the couple and their families and friends, where feasible, I invite the mothers of the marrying couple to come to the altar; I present them with tapers, which they light from the two already lit candles to together ignite the family candle. As the couple's life together proceeds, these two candles signify family and couple union and mutual support. A candle has always been a symbol of the otherworld, the invisible, the mysterious, the ineffable. The soul is the flame of God, Judaism deems. Every Jewish soul is analogous to a lamp as it says in the verse: '*The human soul is God's candle,*' (Proverbs 20:27)

A candle flame brings out the best in us and urges us, as the Buddhist adage goes, to '*commit random acts of kindness*'.

Many interfaith prayers invoke the presence of light to banish the darkness of our own hearts and of the world. I like to take that a step further and salute the shadows that every light creates. Consciously detonating your own light not only provides you with a visual focus but sends out an energy that illuminates unseen and unknown glooms way beyond our awareness. The lighting of a candle marks the beginning of our prayer time; blowing out the flame draws it to a close.

The Irish tradition teaches that, at the moment of your birth, a wax light was lit in Heaven. For the journey of your life, it burns, sometimes steadily in your moments of power and joy, sometimes flickeringly, but still irrepressible and persisting in aching, dismal days. Every celestial candle will vary in size: most candle sizes are long, representing the length of days dealt to you; some are small. When someone dies in Ireland, we never starkly pronounce them dead. Instead, we say, '*Tá a coinneal múchta roimh bhreacadh an lae*' ('Her candle is extinguished before the dawning of the day (of Resurrection)'.

As you light your candle before your morning and night prayers, remember to give thanks for that celestial birthday candle and pray that no one will blow it out until you have completed your work here on earth. In the light of this tradition, when I preside at funeral services, I will invite a family member to blow out the earthly flicker that has now burned its course.

Many interfaith prayers invoke the presence of light to banish the darkness of our own hearts and that of the world. I like to take that a step further and salute the shadows that every light creates. Consciously extinguishing your own light not only provides you with a visual focus but sends out an energy that illuminates unseen and unknown glooms way beyond our awareness.

ÍOMHÁNNA NAOFA: Sacred Images

The second thing to add to your altar are some sacred images and texts. My blessed artists-in-residence include a wooden replica of a Russian icon of Christ the Healer, the original of which lives in the Icon Chapel in Glenstal. This was a birthday gift to me by a dear friend, Mark Patrick Hederman, and, when it catches my eye, it reminds me to give thanks for the gift of all friendships.

Then, there's my Bible, my *Glenstal Book of Prayer*, three medals (one to Mary, one her mother, St Anna, and one to Benedict) and an image of Lord Ganesha. I keep adding and in time removing photos of loved ones past and present and poems that come my way. Have a moveable space on your altar, always in flux, going with the flow.

AN TÚIS: Incense

On the feast of St Benedict – 11 July – in 2016, I moved into my little haven on the boundary of the monastery called Imeall, meaning edge, boundary or threshold in Irish. Another lovely friend, Anna, gifted me a vaporiser and a beautiful wooden Indian box full of essential oils. I am addicted to my ritual of mixing and matching these aromas; every day, a different bouquet mirroring my moods and emotions. A visual delight too, my vaporiser miraculously fluctuates between the seven colours of both rainbow and the chakras. Furthermore, a silent mist rises up as it releases the gentle fragrance.

Though I prefer oils, you may opt for flowers, herbs or an organic perfume – anything that tickles the olefactory sense.

'*Let my prayer rise like incense before you.*' (Psalm 141)

UISCE BEATHA: Water and Sprinklet

Water is a great conduit of prayer, blessing and healing. The Irish word for water is *uisce* – in Irish 'whiskey' is *uisce beatha*, which euphemistically means 'the water of life'. In very moderate doses, perhaps! Holy Water is any H_2O that is meaningful for you, perhaps from the creek at the back of your garden, from a holy well or place sacred to you, even the blessed rainwater that we have by the bucket-load!

Many saints have claimed that water is a great vehicle of protection and keeps evil at bay. St Teresa of Ávila firmly believed this: '*I know by frequent experience that there is nothing which puts the devils to flight like Holy Water*'.

Water is far from inanimate. It is forever shape-shifting from raindrops to icicles, waterfalls to lapping lake water, from mighty torrents and floods to refreshing springs. Yet, we can never catch hold of it or hurt it. Water is crucial to all living things – some organisms are 90 per cent water; we are 60 per cent. Given its symbolic and physical breath, it can have a central place in rituals, shrine spaces and blessings.

Simply gather water that is meaningful to you in a bowl. Then, pick a small branch from a nearby tree or plant, immerse it in the water and sprinkle yourself and your altar space offering a spoken or silent personal prayer or world blessing for protection from evil and guidance.

CLOIGÍN BEAG: A Bell

Bell tolling and chiming, bell ringing and listening, call us to a depth of reverence that is rare. Bells are great reminders that we are about to enter the presence of the sacred; sound thresholds to carry us into the intensity of infinite stillness.

The Celts fashioned their spirituality around sound and particularly bell chime. We have many legends in Ireland that reveal the particular force that bells had. Of the approximately one hundred and twenty round stone towers that dot our landscape, originally constructed between the ninth and twelfth centuries, about twenty remain intact today. These pillars of stone seem to reach up to infinity, and tourists are fascinated as to their function. They are known as *cloigíni*, which means 'little bells'. Monastic ringers would climb to the top and ring their bell out the window to call the brethren to prayer – our Muslim *Adhan*. That the bell was God's gift to humanity is an ancient Irish belief. In the Hindu home, the good beginning is aural. Before *puja* (Sanskrit for gifts to the gods), you ring the bell to alert the deity that you are present and correct.

Bells, as well as stones, work miracles. A saint called Berach lived in Glendalough and chased away demons by ringing his bell. Legend also has it that when Patrick fasted on Croagh Patrick, he flung his bell at some crows who were distracting him from prayer. This Patrician bell – and its finely constructed twelfth-century case – can be seen today in the National Museum of Ireland.

My own bell is a small brass dome with such a sweet tinkle, another birthday gift some years ago from our family friend, poet David Whyte. It is a copy of the same chime he rings during his gatherings. No regular bell-sound here. Once heard, its sonic ring is always a faint echo in my mind long after it has actually sounded.

CÓNAITHEOIRÍ ALTÓRA:
Altar Residents

In creating your altar, you can also add your own odds and ends to it. Make sure to listen to the call of the seasons to attune you to nature's poise along the way – for example, bring in the snowdrops, the crocuses and daffodils in springtime, create your autumn foliage wreath in Advent.

In the Christian tradition, there is the attractive habit of celebrating the various liturgical cycles through colour. So, in Advent, the season before Christmas, and Lent, the season before Easter, the hue of vestments, altar and lectern cloths will be a deep purple that, for me, is the colour of divinity.

AN BEALACH ISTEACH: A Sacred Portal

Before we enter our prayer space, let us create an imaginary lobby, a porch, a green room, where we prepare ourselves to pray.

Theological architecture reflects this, in that most churches, cathedrals, basilicas, temples will have a porch to serve as a threshold between the secular and the sacred. In Christianity, this is called a narthex, an ugly-sounding name but the idea can be adapted – it is a space to get the soul ready for action.

Eastern Christianity has so much to teach us about the home being a mini church. Father and mother are the clergy, and children are the congregation. Every year, the house is blessed or consecrated just as a church might be, complete with great ceremony and blessing of Holy Water.

My own prayer corner in my small living room is overlooked and eyed by a trinity of majestic trees – a beech, an oak and a Spanish chestnut – and the rolling pastures of Glenstal Abbey.

In selecting your own little nook and cranny, we are also following the wise advice of a German–Jewish philosopher who became a Catholic and was murdered in Auschwitz in 1942. Edith Stein, St Teresia Benedicta a Cruce, shared two secrets of what such a recess meant for her: firstly, any tranquil niche to withdraw to reveals the divinity of your inner life; and, secondly, it is the perfect setting to converse all day long with that Divine. In her own words: '*All I need is a quiet corner where I can talk to God each day as if there were nothing else to do*'.

St Paul is surely the patron saint of home altars, 'pray constantly' or 'pray without ceasing' was his advice.

BEANNACHT AR DO SPÁS ALTÓRA:
A sacred space blessing

When I enter my prayer space, I always bless it by sprinkling both it and myself with holy water for protection and cleansing.

Stand silently and comfortably in your precious space for a little time. Ask permission to enter this holy spot and invite the Other to join you and be kind to you. Bid the Divine to help you open your heart and soul to what wants to be heard this morning or evening, perhaps by ringing a bell, as in Hinduism. George Herbert, the seventeenth-century metaphysical poet, compared prayer to the soul speaking; it is the *'soul in paraphrase'*. In other words, to pray is to do our soul work. Care of the soul is prayer care.

CÚINNE CIÚIN:

Ritual to Welcome in a Quiet Corner

Below is my ritual for welcoming in a silent space. Imagine that you are stepping into a *currach*, the traditional ancient Irish basic wooden boat over which animal skins were stretched. In early Irish Christianity, small bands of monks would step aboard and launch into the unknown waters – the important detail here is that they didn't have any oars. They knew and trusted that the Divine would steer their *currachs* to the perfect journey's end where they were to begin their mission.

When you enter your altar space, you are stepping into *your* saintly vessel without an oar or a compass, knowing that during this silent prayer time, you will be navigated to the nameless shore that your soul is yearning to visit on that day.

DO PHAIDIR FÉIN: Praying in Your Own Words

It took me a long time to create my personal prayer to the Divine. So now I want to encourage you to design and conceive your personal, private 'devotion recipe' that is an honest conversation with your *anam chara*, your trusted supporter of your own choosing. I say this prayer at the beginning of my prayer ritual every day. I encourage you to create your own personal prayer, one that feels special to you. The language does not need to be overly formal; what's most important is that it sets the intention for your ritual.

I've written below my ingredients for my daily conversation with my holy ally, St Anna, mother of Mary, Mother of God. She makes no appearance in the four gospels of the New Testament. Her narrative is told in what's called an apocryphal gospel of St James. She has been my 'helper' saint and has inspired me greatly for many years. I begin by addressing her and expressing thanks to her for her presence:

❈❈❈❈❈❈❈❈❈❈❈❈❈❈❈❈❈❈❈❈❈❈❈

O dearest St Anna, I am so grateful for the grace of your company in my life.

❈❈❈❈❈❈❈❈❈❈❈❈❈❈❈❈❈❈❈❈❈❈❈

Then I will elaborate on her role:

❈❈❈❈❈❈❈❈❈❈❈❈❈❈❈❈❈❈❈❈❈❈❈

Mother of Mary, mother of God, so grandmother both of God and the Son of God, and my grandmother and friend too.

❈❈❈❈❈❈❈❈❈❈❈❈❈❈❈❈❈❈❈❈❈❈❈

Then my petition to her: here I smile at the humanity of it all! As we say in Ireland, butter someone up and then slip in the nifty request!

✺❀✺❀✺❀✺❀✺❀✺❀✺❀✺❀✺❀✺❀✺❀✺❀✺❀✺❀✺❀✺

May you shower your maternal wisdom and courage upon me as I struggle today with …

✺❀✺❀✺❀✺❀✺❀✺❀✺❀✺❀✺❀✺❀✺❀✺❀✺❀✺❀✺❀✺

Then, I will aim to be generous and detached to assure her that no matter what her decision might be, I will never cease to call upon her and to accept her will.

✺❀✺❀✺❀✺❀✺❀✺❀✺❀✺❀✺❀✺❀✺❀✺❀✺❀✺❀✺❀✺

Even though, Anna, this should require a miracle, I will never cease to call on you and to praise you daily.

✺❀✺❀✺❀✺❀✺❀✺❀✺❀✺❀✺❀✺❀✺❀✺❀✺❀✺❀✺❀✺

A final prayer word or phrase seals the offering.

✺❀✺❀✺❀✺❀✺❀✺❀✺❀✺❀✺❀✺❀✺❀✺❀✺❀✺❀✺❀✺

Amen, Allellujah, in God's own time, namaste. Nothing will be impossible for God, L'Shalom, Magnificat, grá mo chroí thú (you are the love of my heart).

The second tool for creating a prayer is setting the music of your soul to text. Give it words and let the song sing for itself. Put words upon what you feel deeply about.

LÉIGH AMACH ÓS ÁRD: Read Out Loud

A word here about heightening these prayers you are about to meet. Prayer, as pure vibration and resonance, is the conversation I want to have with you now. If at all possible, I urge you to read all your prayers *out loud.*

The intention and belief of early authors was that the silent, optical word would live and have its primary power through the actual sound of it. In many languages, including Hebrew, the verb 'to read' also means 'to give voice to'. To verbalise a text is to hear what the eye sees. The word becomes tattooed on the soul through oration.

The poem prayers that I have chosen in this book are all hearer-friendly, and reciting them is a prerequisite for access to familiarity and intimacy. A twentieth-century Benedictine monk, Jean Leclercq, describes this listening to the 'voice of the pages' as in a real acoustic reading 'one understands only what one hears'. Poem-prayers are meant to be converted into outcry and said in a distinct, compelling tone.

The Book of Revelation, a very audio-centric tome, was understandably Emily Dickinson's favourite scripture. '*Blessed is the one who reads aloud the words of the prophecy, and blessed are those who hear ... it.*' (Rev. 1:3)

Since it is a biological truth that we can hear our own voices as we talk, because there is a direct neural connection between the larynx and the ear, we are doubly blessed as both speaker and listener! Voicing, chanting, singing bring our prayers home to ourselves and to God.

As you read aloud the poems and prayers during your ritual, say the words slowly and consciously, enabling the lesson to come through. Just as in the ancient spiritual practice of *Lectio Divina* – Divine Reading – let a word or phrase speak out to you and pierce your heart. Repeat it over and over aloud, letting the syllables roll onto your lips. Ask why this prayer has come to you at this time. Step aside to allow the Spirit to speak to you. I call this *Audio Divina* – Divine Listening.

In the silence after, address and thank the author, whoever that might be.

ANGELIC PRESENCES

Call in that caring presence around you that we call angels who are always near 'lest you strike your foot against a stone' to mind you and keep you safe. A shielding force who shares all your secrets, your worries, your anxieties, and wants you to know of her presence, and longs for constant conversation with you. There is an angel for everyone and in everything around us. Patrick Kavanagh communed with *'the angel of the mountainy places'*. This is not a New Age arrival. Angels are very powerful in the Old Testament and in all religions but we turn our back on them. There is a Jewish proverb, 'Before every person there marches an angel proclaiming, "Behold, the image of God."' Miracles happen and, put another way, because our angels are constantly working overtime for us, the ordinary merges into the extra ordinary.

※*※*※*※*※*※*※*※*※*※*※*※*※*※*※

'O, Guardian angel, although I sometimes fail to greet you, do not overlook me in your loving care.'
I love this Irish angelic breastplate. Although not mentioned by name, the honoured angel in the Muslim, Jewish and Christian faiths is always the 'Noble angel'. Profoundly, the invocation to Archangel Michael walks alongside, coping with the strange contradiction where our good and evil personas meet.

'A Aingeal Uasal, a Aingeal Dé,
cabhraigh liom ar feadh an lae.
Bí le m'ais go síoraí dlúth,
Ná lig don diabhal mé 'chur amú'.

'O, noble angel of God, help me throughout this day. Be forever firm standing beside me. Do not let the [d]evil lead me astray.' The Jewish tradition has its own marvellous integration of angels. I learned this blessing from a great friend singer in Jerusalem, Ruth Wieder Magan. We sang this many times together in Ireland and Israel.

⁕⁕⁕⁕⁕⁕⁕⁕⁕⁕⁕⁕⁕⁕⁕⁕⁕⁕⁕⁕⁕⁕⁕

Every Friday evening on returning home from the Synagogue, the angels are welcomed in on the Eve of the Shabbat.

⁕⁕⁕⁕⁕⁕⁕⁕⁕⁕⁕⁕⁕⁕⁕⁕⁕⁕⁕⁕⁕⁕⁕

Shalom aleikhem, malakhei hasharet,
malakhei elyon, Mimelekh malkhei ham'lakhim, hakadosh
barukh hu. Peace be with you, ministering angels, messengers of
the Most High,
Messengers of the King of Kings, the Holy One, Blessed be He.
Bar-khuni l'shalom, malakhei hashalom, malakhei elyon,
Mimelekh malakhei ham'lakhim, hakadosh barukh hu. Bless me
with peace, messengers of peace, messengers of the Most High,
Messengers of the King of Kings, the Holy One, Blessed be He.

⁕⁕⁕⁕⁕⁕⁕⁕⁕⁕⁕⁕⁕⁕⁕⁕⁕⁕⁕⁕⁕⁕⁕

There are two recurring motifs in angel prayer: one is of invocation; the other is the circle of friendship which angels hold out to us – unexpected, surprising friendship almost akin to love. Past and future, time spent and time yet to be spent form no barrier between us and them. I am living proof of this subtle presence just this morning. As I was assembling this little potpourri of angel prayers, the postman called with a handwritten letter from a dear friend of mine in Buffalo, Ansie Baird. It contained a poem that she had just written and signed it to me: "for Nóirín – love, Ansie." A still graveyard heron two days in a row transforms Ansie's way of being in the humdrum vacant world in such a way as to represent a harbinger of petite sanctity. Let awareness be the great gift of your guardian angels. Angels call out and sing; there are secret worlds hidden in the simplest of things. Go and discover these new possibilities of jewels buried in your familiar, predictable backyard.

CALL IN YOUR ANGELS

'Where are my angels, anyway?
A great blue heron lurks or
Considers his life on a leafy branch
Of a capacious tree bending
Over the creek in the cemetery

Just across the street from me.
He was there yesterday, preening
His long beak tucked in his
Lavish chest of gray-blue feathers,
Monk-like, stolid and imposing,
Gazing my way. Today, when
I return, there he is again,
On the same branch of the tree.
Damn tree. Good God,
Is he dead or something?
No, he turns his head
Watching as wild ducks
Gather in a pack to take wing.

He must be waiting for me.
Perhaps he's one of my angels,
A kind of intercessor
Between my vacancy and
That which is abundant.
I'm not inclined to ask him
For a blessing but his presence
In this graveyard feels auspicious,
Transforming one more bleak
Evening into something maybe
Just a tiny bit holy.

※＊※＊※＊※＊※＊※＊※＊※＊※＊※＊※＊※＊※

AN TSEACHTAIN
I bPAIDIR :
Seven-Day Rituals

Mornings and evenings are the great praying times of the day in all faith traditions. For example, in India, the day is made up of eight *praharas*, divisions that punctuate every twenty-four hours. The first *prahara* of the day begins at sunrise, and the fourth ends at sunset. Every *prahara* has its own devotional sound, mantra or prayer.

Classical music celebrates the early and late evening as a time to awaken to the spirit of the hidden night through particular ragas or melodies.

So, first of all, we will introduce morning and evening prayer stops for every day of the week.

Incidentally, the Christian tradition regards Sunday as the first day of the week, but my praying week always begins on Monday and ends on a high with Sunday – the day of the Creator and Resurrection.

Chakramental and Sacramental Routine

A particular line from St Paul formed the source of my daily piecing together of chakramental and sacramental routine. In the first letter to the people of Corinth (Chapter 6), Paul reminds us: '*Do you not know that your body is a temple of the Holy Spirit within you, which you have from God … therefore glorify God in your body*'.

The Sanskrit names are so much more beautiful than our English translation so do not lose the opportunity to foster the unseen blessings of the chakras and savour the 'a' vowel sound personality of each as you call it by name aloud.

- Monday honours the root chakra, *Muladhara,* at the base of your spine; its colour is red and its gift is grounding and steadiness.

- Tuesday, I bless the sacral chakra, *Swadhisthana,* just below the lower abdomen. Tuesday's colour is orange and when in balance, our egocentric, self-centred love interweaves with a generous, unconditional love, which is of more of a divine nature. Ancient Greece labelled these two love opposites as Eros – the need and desire that distances us from God – and Agape – the highest form of love that transcends all and unites us with the transcendental.

- Wednesday's energy wheel resides in your upper abdomen. Called *Manipura,* the solar plexus, is the shelter of self-confidence and control. Yellow is the colour here.

- Thursday, *Anahata,* with its four 'a's, is heart work, dyed in green and all about tenderness and compassion.

- Friday, called *Vishuddhi,* rests in the throat, ready to emerge when we speak and listen. Pay attention to your throat chakrament and you shall hear with ear of the heart. The throat chakra is tinted turquoise, a blending of tranquil blue and wild red.

- Saturday, *Ajna,* is between your ears and your eyes and here the colour is beautiful indigo – an intermingling of blue and violet. Be grateful to this chakrament for your creativity and imagination.

- On Sunday, the vital integration of spiritual poise and balance is called, again around a quartet of 'a's – *Sahasrara.* Aptly called the Crown, I tag it the *prayer 'seacht roth'* – the key chakra that opens the gate to Heaven on earth.

Sahasrara is where your soul is, the sure location of the meeting point between you and the Divine force. It is exactly the locus of the art of homecoming to your highest and best self, the midwife to the birth of your soul to The Other. There are two colours connected to this Crown chakra; violet and a bright white. Violet or purple is my favourite shade. When we come to search for God, let this little imagined crack in our skull be opencd wide in consciousness, sprinkling the crevices of love with awe and mystery. All you need is here for you to become a pure vessel for the grace of your deepest call; now on this seventh day of rest, you have come full circle to the unfinished and imperfect in your life. Pick up the receiver and listen. The circle of protection is sealed around you since both these extremities of energy wheels – the root and the crown – are energetically connected.

NAOIMH AN LAE: Saints of the Day

I also have my own preference of committing each day of the week to a particular deity, one from the Irish tradition and one from India where every day there is dedicated to a saint from the Hindu pantheon. Below are these allegiances and chakras:

- Dé Luain: Monday – The Angels/Lord Shiva

- Dé Máirt: Tuesday – Anna (mother of Mary)/Lord Ganesha/Lord Hanuman

- Dé Céadaoine: Wednesday – Brigid (Celtic goddess and Christian saint)/Lord Krishna

- Daordaoine: Thursday – St Nicholas (patron saint of Russia, buried in Kilkenny Ireland)/Lord Vishnu

- Dé hAoine: Friday – Christ (tradition holds that the human cosmic figure died on this day)/Mother Goddess Lakshmi

- Dé Sathairn: Saturday – Muire/Mary (mother of God)/ The Divine Feminine/Lord Shani

- Dé Domhnaigh: Sunday – God the Creator of new Life and Resurrection/Lord Surya

CRUTH NA SEACHTAINE:
The shape of the prayer session

As outlined earlier, bless yourself and your prayer space upon entering it with a sprinkle of holy water. Then stand comfortably and silently in this space for a little time.

Then light the candle on your altar to invite in Divine light and presence and to recall our own ever-burning flame in the heavens. When you light your candle, you are in harmony with that celestial flame. Each prayer stop begins and ends with the lighting and extinguishing of a candle.

AN GLAOCH CHUN URNAÍ:
Opening Call to Prayer

The first prayer of each session is said three times whilst you bless yourself on your lips. This can reflect your own experience and may take the form of a sign of a cross, a heart image, star of David, an initial, whatever. The same prayer is repeated each day in both prayer stops.

❀❀❀❀❀❀❀❀❀❀❀❀❀❀❀❀❀❀❀❀

MAIDIN: Morning

'Lord, open my lips and my mouth will declare your praise.'
(Psalm 51)
Repeat this three times and make a blessing on your lips.

❀❀❀❀❀❀❀❀❀❀❀❀❀❀❀❀❀❀❀❀

TRÁTHNÓNA: Evening

'O God, come to my aid, O Lord make haste to help me.'
(Psalm 70)

SLIOCHT NAOFA: A Scripture Quotation

Many wisdom texts are drawn upon in the following section and some Psalm snippets inspire us from the classic ancient Hebrew songs of the Old Testament. Why the Psalms? Just two of the many references suffice to justify their inclusion.

First of all, St Augustine of Hippo who summed up the entire 150 psalms: '*If the psalm prays, you pray; if it laments, you lament; if it exults, you rejoice; if it hopes, you hope; if it fears, you fear. Everything written here is a mirror for us*'. (Augustine's *Confessions*)

Secondly, St Jerome, a biblical scholar from the fourth century, was asked by Laeta, one of the many women to whom he gave spiritual direction, where she should begin when negotiating Scripture. Without a moment's hesitation, Jerome pointed to the Book of Psalms – therein, he told her she would not only study Scripture, but she would learn to pray.

AN PHAIDIR CHIÚIN: Silent prayer

This will vary according to your schedule and how much time you have for prayer. Ring a bell or strike a chime as you imaginatively step into your own oarless *currach* of trust and hope. Let your busy mind float adrift for a spell. Ring the bell again to herald your arrival at the shore of the day's destiny.

IDIRGHUÍ PEARSANTA:

Your Personal Prayer

Whatever intuition came to you, commit now to prayer – either aloud or in your heart. Firstly, respect your own moment of need, then the needs of someone close or, indeed, not so dear to you and, finally, extend that blessing out to the universe, particularly those war-torn lands and starving peoples.

DÁN DÉ AN LÁ – Sacred Verse of the Day

To seal your prayer, to end well and, before you turn to face either the day or night, say this poem that, in time, you might learn off by heart.

BEANNACHT DEIRIGH: Final Blessing

Repeat the blessing of the Holy Ones of the day and chakra.

MÚCHADH AN CHOINNEALL:

Extinguish Your Earthly Candle.

ANÁL d'ANAM: The breath of your soul

A final consideration before we begin our daily ritual is about breath – by far the most crucial and effective tool for ritual building.

As you begin your prayer session, stand, kneel or make yourself comfortable where you sit. Close your eyes. Breathe in and out slowly and deliberately, aware of the subtle body movements in your stomach and chest. Expanding as you take in the air around you, letting go as you exhale. Revel in the miracle of it all, and speak kindly to each inhalation and exhalation, something we do at least 22,000 times a day. As you breathe in, feel the pleasant lure into your heart. Breathing out, lighten up and slow down. Build on your breath gradually growing aware of your path towards transformation and growth.

Notice and speak kindly to any corner of your body that might be in pain or uncomfortable. Note, on the other hand, all of the other regions within you that are at ease. Your body is now at one with your soul.

Listen to your breath, inhaling through your nose and exhaling through the mouth; your nostrils singing its breathy song and your mouth responding with its own little wind of release. This is a network of sounds, a call and response, that we don't normally listen to, so savour it. What is happening is that the rhythm of your life force is retrieving its primal connection with the ancient three-fold meaning of the Greek *pneuma* and Hebrew *ruach* – wind, breath and spirit.

As I inhale, I like to think of the dawning of a new day and then exhale with the ease and surety of the dusk. Then pause for a little after each in-breath; a temporary halt that symbolises midday before you let your breath out.

You may well want to spend additional time beyond your prayer ritual and consider one or other of these responses.

• Breathing in: I pray to be minded in joy.

• Breathing out: I pray to let go of any anger.

• Breathing in: peace comes at once.

• Breathing out: the air of anxiety evaporates.

• Breathing in: I usher in a deep prayerful happiness.

• Breathing out: the voice of sadness is silenced.

• Breathing in: compassion, I smile in praise.

• Breathing out: the plague of lonesomeness, I smile in prayer.

When you feel that the time is right, open your eyes and look all around you, tenderly swivelling your head from side to side. Know that you can repeat this ritual of prayerful breathing to drive away the inevitable uncertainties and disquiets of being in this world.

STAD PAIDIR AN LAE AGUS TRÁTHNÓNA:
Morning and Evening Prayer

DÉ LUAIN: Monday

The Angels
Maladhara – Lord Shiva – Root (Seacht Roth) Chakra

MAIDIN: Morning

AN CHOINEALL BEO: The Living Candle

Light your candle, and prepare for the ritual that follows.

AN GLAOCH CHUN URNAÍ: Opening Call to Prayer

Lord, open my lips and my mouth will declare your praise.
(Psalm 51)

Repeat this three times and make a blessing on your lips.

SLIOCHT NAOFA: A Scripture Quotation

May I be a guard for those who need protection
A guide for those on the path
A boat, a raft, a bridge for those who wish to cross the flood.
Shantideva, Indian Buddhist sage 700 CE

AN PAIDIR CHIÚIN: Silent Prayer

The timing here will vary according to your schedule. Ring a bell or a chime as you imaginatively step into your own oarless *currach* of trust and hope. Let your busy mind float adrift for a spell. Ring the bell to herald your arrival at the shore of the day's destiny.

AN PAIDIR PHEARSANTA: Personal Prayer

Whatever intuition came to you during your *paidir chiúin*, commit now to prayer – either aloud or in your heart; honouring your own moment of need, then the needs of someone close or indeed not so dear to you and, finally, extending that blessing out to the universe, particularly those war-torn lands and starving peoples.

DÁN DÉ AN LÁ: Sacred Verse of the Day

Some keep the Sabbath going to Church –
I keep it, staying at Home –
With a Bobolink for a Chorister –
And an Orchard, for a Dome –

Some keep the Sabbath in Surplice –
I, just wear my Wings –
And instead of tolling the Bell for Church,
Our little Sexton – sings.

God preaches, a noted Clergyman –
And the sermon is never long,
So instead of getting to Heaven, at last –
I'm going, all along.

Emily Dickinson

BEANNACHT DEIRIGH: Final Blessing

O Angel of God, my guardian dear,
To whom God's love commits me here.
Ever this day be at my side,
To light and guard, to rule and guide.
Amen.

May Lord Shiva, bestower of goodness, be praised.

May the power of the Root chakra – Maladhara – bring me stability and groundedness today, so that I may vibrate with the rhythm and vibration of the earth. In that energetic dance with the cosmos, may I be renewed in goodness and kindness to be shared with all whom I encounter this day.

MÚCHADH AN CHOINEALL BEO: Quenching the Live Candle

Know that even as you blow out your *coinneal domhanda* (earthly flame), your blessed angelic light continues to flicker for you this day.

TRÁTHNÓNA: Evening

AN CHOINEALL BEO: The Living Candle
Light your candle, and prepare for the ritual that follows.

AN GLAOCH CHUN URNAÍ: Opening Call to Prayer
O God, come to my aid, O Lord make haste to help me.
(Psalm 70)

Make the sign of the cross as you say this.

SLIOCHT NAOFA: A Scripture Quotation
My soul glorifies the Lord, my spirit rejoices in God my Saviour.
For he has looked with favour on his humble servant and, from
this day onwards, all generations will call me blessed. For the
Almighty has done great things for me and holy is God's name.
Mary's Canticle (Luke 1:46–55)

AN PAIDIR CHIÚIN: Silent Prayer
The timing here will vary according to your schedule. Ring a
bell or a chime as you imaginatively step into your own oarless

currach of trust and hope. Let your busy mind float adrift for a spell. Ring the bell to herald your arrival at the shore of the day's destiny.

AN PAIDIR PHEARSANTA: Personal Prayer

Whatever intuition or memo came to you during your *paidir chiúin*, commit now to prayer – either aloud or in your heart; honouring your own moment of need, then the needs of someone close or indeed not so dear to you and, finally, extending that blessing out to the universe, particularly those war-torn lands and starving peoples.

DÁN DÉ AN LÁ: Sacred Verse of the Day

God is there in these moments of rest and can give us in a single instant exactly what we need. Then the rest of the day can take its course, under the same effort and strain, perhaps, but in peace. And when night comes, and you look back over the day and see how fragmentary everything has been, and how much you planned that has gone undone, and all the reasons you have to be embarrassed and ashamed: just take everything exactly as it is, put it in God's hands and leave it with Him. Then you will be able to rest in Him – really rest – and start the next day as a new life.

Edith Stein, Judaeo–Christian saint

BEANNACHT DEIRIGH: Final Blessing

Blessing of the Holy Ones of the day and chakra

As I end this day in peace, may the Maladhara at the base of my spine keep me physically and spiritually upright, steady and strong.

O angelic forces, watch over me, my loved ones and the universe this night.

Lord Shiva, free us from the prison of earthly attachment and bring us safely through this miniature death of sleep without fear or anxiety.

MÚCHADH AN CHOINNEALL: Extinguish your Earthly Candle

Knowing that, although you are blowing out your *coinneal domhanda* (earthly flame), your blessed angelic light continues to flicker for you this night.

DÉ MÁIRT: Tuesday

St Anna (mother of Mary, the mother of God)

Swadhisthana – Lord Ganesha, Lord Hanuman – Sacral Chakra

Maidin: Morning

AN CHOINEALL BEO: The Living Candle

Light your candle, and prepare for the ritual that follows.

AN GLAOCH CHUN URNAÍ: Opening Call to Prayer

Lord, open my lips and my mouth will declare your praise.
(Psalm 51)

Repeat this three times and make a blessing on your lips.

SLIOCHT NAOFA: A Scripture Quotation

If there is righteousness in the heart, there will be beauty in the character.

If there is beauty in the character, there will be harmony in the home.

If there is harmony in the home, there will be order in the nation.

If there is order in the nation, there will be peace in the world.

The Analects of Confucius, 550 BCE

AN PAIDIR CHIÚIN: Silent Prayer

The timing here will vary according to your schedule. Ring a bell or a chime as you imaginatively step into your own oarless *currach* of trust and hope. Let your busy mind float adrift for a spell. Ring the bell to herald your arrival at the shore of the day's destiny.

AN PAIDIR PHEARSANTA: Personal Prayer

Whatever intuition or memo came to you during your *paidir chiúin*, commit now to prayer – either aloud or in your heart; honouring your own moment of need, then the needs

of someone close or indeed not so dear to you and, finally, extending that blessing out to the universe, particularly those war-torn lands and starving peoples.

DÁN DÉ AN LÁ: Sacred Verse of the Day

Éirím suas le Dia (I arise with God)
Go n-éirí Dia liom (May God arise with me)
Lámh Dé i mo thimpeall (The hand of God all around me)
Ag suí 's ag luí 's ag éirí dhom (As I sit, as I lie, as I arise now)
Irish Traditional

BEANNACHT DEIRIGH: Final Blessing

Anna of Tuesday, legend tells us that you self-taught your daughter Mary all of the Jewish Scriptures. Teach us now how to pray. In Ireland, a grandmother is called *mamó*. So *mamó*, we place ourselves under your care this morning, and remain with us throughout the coming hours.

Lord Ganesha, you are the one who removes obstacles. Help me today to persist and survive any difficulties that may arise.

May the sacral chakra – Swadhisthana – come alive today to remind me to love deeply and to rise above negativity and confrontation.

❋❋❋❋❋❋❋❋❋❋❋❋❋❋❋❋❋

MÚCHADH AN CHOINNEALL: Extinguish Your Earthly Candle

Knowing that, although you are blowing out your *coinneal domhanda* (earthly flame), your blessed angelic light continues to flicker for you this night.

TRÁTHNÓNA: Evening

AN CHOINEALL BEO: The Living Candle

Light your candle, and prepare for the ritual that follows.

❋❋❋❋❋❋❋❋❋❋❋❋❋❋❋❋❋

AN GLAOCH CHUN URNAÍ: Opening Call to Prayer

O God, come to my aid, O Lord make haste to help me.
(Psalm 70)

Make the sign of the cross as you say this.

❋❋❋❋❋❋❋❋❋❋❋❋❋❋❋❋❋

SLIOCHT NAOFA: A Scripture Quotation

In your power, in your thought, all things are abundant. Tonight, I will sleep beneath your feet, O Lord of the mountains and valleys, ruler of the trees and vines. I will rest in your love, with you protecting me as a father protects his children, with you watching over me as a mother watches over her children. Then tomorrow the sun will rise and I will not know where I am, but I know that you will guide my footsteps.

Native American, Sioux

AN PAIDIR CHIÚIN: Silent Prayer

The timing here will vary according to your schedule. Ring a bell or a chime as you imaginatively step into your own oarless *currach* of trust and hope. Let your busy mind float adrift for a spell. Ring the bell to herald your arrival at the shore of the day's destiny.

AN PAIDIR PHEARSANTA: Personal Prayer

Whatever intuition or memo came to you during your *paidir chiúin*, commit now to prayer – either aloud or in your heart; honouring your own moment of need, then the needs of someone close or indeed not so dear to you and, finally, extend that blessing out to the universe, particularly those war-torn lands and starving peoples.

❋⁂❋⁂❋⁂❋⁂❋⁂❋⁂❋⁂❋⁂❋⁂❋⁂❋⁂❋

DÁN DÉ AN LÁ: Sacred Verse of the Day

As shadows fall and daylight dies,
Renew your gift of peace.
Be with us as we close our eyes,
Let all our troubles cease.
Though we may sleep, stay in our hearts,
Keep your love there ablaze.
When darkness of the night departs,
We'll rise to sing your praise.

Glenstal Abbey Compline

❋⁂❋⁂❋⁂❋⁂❋⁂❋⁂❋⁂❋⁂❋⁂❋⁂❋⁂❋

BEANNACHT DEIRIGH: Final Blessing

Mamó Anna, I am grateful to you for the little secret surprises that you sent to me this day as I take stock this evening. May you continue to shower me with dream gifts and wonder this night.

Lord Ganesha, saint of hospitality and problem solver, provide me and my family with protection and an abundance of food, physical and spiritual.

May the creative energy of the sacral – Swadhisthana – fuel our imagination this night. Herein lies the source of sexuality and reproduction, and we remember all this evening who struggle with conception and creativity of any sort.

MÚCHADH AN CHOINNEALL:

Extinguish Your Earthly Candle

Knowing that, although you are blowing out your *coinneal domhanda* (earthly flame), your blessed angelic light continues to flicker for you this night.

DÉ CÉADAOINE: Wednesday

St Brigit (Celtic triple goddess and Christian saint, patron saint of Ireland)

Manipura – Lord Krishna – Solar Plexus Chakra

Maidin: Morning

AN CHOINEALL BEO: The Living Candle

Light your candle, and prepare for the ritual that follows.

AN GLAOCH CHUN URNAÍ: Opening Call to Prayer

Lord, open my lips and my mouth will declare your praise.
(Psalm 51)

Repeat this three times and make a blessing on your lips.

SLIOCHT NAOFA: A Scripture Quotation

May I be a lamp in the darkness
A resting place for the weary
A healing medicine for all who are sick
A vase of plenty, a tree of miracles
And for the boundless multitudes of living beings, may I
bring sustenance and awakening, enduring like the earth
and sky until all beings are freed from sorrow and all are
awakened. Shantideva, Indian Buddhist sage 700 CE

AN PAIDIR CHIÚIN: Silent Prayer

The timing here will vary according to your schedule. Ring a bell or a chime as you imaginatively step into your own oarless *currach* of trust and hope. Let your busy mind float adrift for a spell. Ring the bell to herald your arrival at the shore of the day's destiny.

AN PAIDIR PHEARSANTA: Personal Prayer

Whatever intuition or memo came to you during your *paidir chiúin*, commit now to prayer – either aloud or in your heart; honouring your own moment of need, then the needs of someone close or indeed not so dear to you and, finally, extending that blessing out to the universe, particularly those war-torn lands and starving peoples.

❁❁❁❁❁❁❁❁❁❁❁❁❁❁❁❁❁❁❁❁❁

DÁN DÉ AN LÁ
– Sacred Verse of the Day

Then a priestess said, speak to us of prayer and he answered, saying …
God listens not to your words save when He Himself utters them
through your lips …
Kahlil Gibran, *The Garden of the Prophet*

❁❁❁❁❁❁❁❁❁❁❁❁❁❁❁❁❁❁❁❁❁

※∗※∗※∗※∗※∗※∗※∗※∗※∗※∗※∗※∗※∗※∗※

BEANNACHT DEIRIGH: Final Blessing

Bridgit, triple goddess and Christian saint, spread around us your mantle of healing, poetry and transformation today. Your generosity, your commitment to justice, I promise to take with me in all the challenges I may be confronted with today.

Lord Krishna, the original and supreme Hindu God, make my path favourable and auspicious. Bestow this blessing on all whom I meet and address this day.

The Solar Plexus – Manipura – energy is one of self-love and care. I pray that I can mind myself, be good to myself, be non-judgemental this day.

※∗※∗※∗※∗※∗※∗※∗※∗※∗※∗※∗※∗※∗※∗※

MÚCHADH AN CHOINNEALL:

Extinguish Your Earthly Candle

Knowing that, although you are blowing out your *coinneal domhanda* (earthly flame), your blessed angelic light continues to flicker for you this day.

TRÁTHNÓNA: *Evening*
AN CHOINEALL BEO: The Living Candle

Light your candle, and prepare for the ritual that follows.

✻❊✻❊✻❊✻❊✻❊✻❊✻❊✻❊✻❊✻❊✻❊✻❊✻❊✻❊✻❊

O God, come to my aid, O Lord make haste to help me.
(Psalm 70)

Make the sign of the cross as you say this.

✻❊✻❊✻❊✻❊✻❊✻❊✻❊✻❊✻❊✻❊✻❊✻❊✻❊✻❊✻❊

SLIOCHT NAOFA: A Scripture Quotation
Gladness of heart in life is what gives length of days ...
Beguile your cares, console your heart, chase sorrow away; for
sorrow has been the ruin of many and is of no use to anybody.
Ecclesiasticus/Sirach (30: 21–29)

✻❊✻❊✻❊✻❊✻❊✻❊✻❊✻❊✻❊✻❊✻❊✻❊✻❊✻❊✻❊

AN PAIDIR CHIÚIN: Silent prayer
The timing here will vary according to your schedule. Ring a
bell or a chime as you imaginatively step into your own oarless
currach of trust and hope. Let your busy mind float adrift for
a spell. Ring the bell to herald your arrival at the shore of the
day's destiny.

AN PAIDIR PHEARSANTA: Personal Prayer
Whatever intuition or memo came to you during your *paidir*
chiúin, commit now to prayer – either aloud or in your
heart; honouring your own moment of need, then the needs

of someone close or indeed not so dear to you and, finally, extending that blessing out to the universe, particularly those war-torn lands and starving peoples.

✺❋✺❋✺❋✺❋✺❋✺❋✺❋✺❋✺❋✺❋✺❋✺❋✺

DÁN DÉ AN LÁ: Sacred Verse of the Day

O make me wholly Thine!
Thy love to me impart,
And let Thy holy spirit shine
For ever on my heart!
Anne Brontë, excerpt from 'Confidence'

✺❋✺❋✺❋✺❋✺❋✺❋✺❋✺❋✺❋✺❋✺❋✺❋✺

BEANNACHT DEIRIGH: Final Blessing

A Bhríd chaoin, beannaigh mise agus mo chlann is t'oíche (Oh gentle Brigit, bless me and my family this night). Spread your peace among us this evening and may we rest in your assurance that 'the happy heart is true'.

Hare Krishna, Hare Rama, fill me with your blessing of Divine awareness and consciousness this evening that I may rise refreshed and renewed in your Higher Power to do your will.

This evening, I honour the Solar Plexus – Manipura – where self-care resides. Firstly in body, by eating and drinking in moderation before I retire. Secondly, minding my soul through connecting now with my Higher Self and Power.

MÚCHADH AN CHOINNEALL:

Extinguish Your Earthly Candle

Knowing that, although you are blowing out your *coinneal domhanda* (earthly flame), your blessed angelic light continues to flicker for you this night.

DAORDAOINE: Thursday

St Nicholas (patron saint of Russia)

Anahata – Lord Vishnu – Heart Chakra

Maidin: Morning

AN CHOINEALL BEO: The Living Candle

Light your candle, and prepare for the ritual that follows.

AN GLAOCH CHUN URNAÍ: Opening Call to Prayer

Lord, open my lips and my mouth will declare your praise.
(Psalm 51)

Repeat this three times and make a blessing on your lips.

SLIOCHT NAOFA: A Scripture Quotation

Come to me all you that are weary and are carrying heavy burdens, and I will give you rest. Take my yoke upon you and learn from me; for I am humble in heart, and you will find rest for your souls. For my yoke is easy and by burden light.
Matthew 11

AN PAIDIR CHIÚIN: Silent Prayer

The timing here will vary according to your schedule. Ring a bell or a chime as you imaginatively step into your own oarless *currach* of trust and hope. Let your busy mind float adrift for a spell. Ring the bell to herald your arrival at the shore of the day's destiny.

AN PAIDIR PHEARSANTA: Personal Prayer

Whatever intuition or memo came to you during your *paidir chiúin*, commit now to prayer – either aloud or in your heart; honouring your own moment of need, then the needs of someone close or indeed not so dear to you and, finally, extending that blessing out to the universe, particularly those war-torn lands and starving peoples.

DÁN DÉ AN LÁ: Sacred Verse of the Day

Let every wind that blows drop honey.
Let the rivers and streams recreate honey.
Let all our medicines turn honey.
Let the dawn and evening be full of honey.
Let the dark particles be converted to honey.
Our nourisher, this sky above, be full of honey.
Let our trees be honey.
Let the Sun be honey.
Let our cows secrete honey.
Rig Veda (1: 90: 6–8)

BEANNACHT DEIRIGH: Final Blessing

Nicholas, saint of generosity, may I be open-hearted today in my thoughts, words, deeds and contacts. In Russia, they say that '*if God dies, we'll always have St Nicholas*'. I believe in your bounty, help get rid of my smallness of mind.

Lord Vishnu, protector of the universe, may our troubled world know your healing care as we commit the cosmic chaos and pains of our times. Show me the path that I may take to alleviate suffering around me today.

The heart – Anahata – is the locus of love, connection and forgiveness. Teach me today to love what is good, to connect with what will nourish, and to forgive myself and others for any wrongs, real or imagined, that I carry.

❃✳❃✳❃✳❃✳❃✳❃✳❃✳❃✳❃✳❃✳❃✳❃✳❃✳❃✳❃

MÚCHADH AN CHOINNEALL: Extinguish Your Earthly Candle

Knowing that, although you are blowing out your *coinneal domhanda* (earthly flame), your blessed angelic light continues to flicker for you this night.

TRÁTHNÓNA: Evening
AN CHOINEALL BEO: The Living Candle
Light your candle, and prepare for the ritual that follows.

❃✳❃✳❃✳❃✳❃✳❃✳❃✳❃✳❃✳❃✳❃✳❃✳❃✳❃✳❃

AN GLAOCH CHUN URNAÍ: Opening Call to Prayer

O God, come to my aid, O Lord make haste to help me.
(Psalm 70)

Make the sign of the cross as you say this.

✺ ❊ ✺ ❊ ✺ ❊ ✺ ❊ ✺ ❊ ✺ ❊ ✺ ❊ ✺ ❊ ✺ ❊ ✺ ❊ ✺ ❊ ✺

SLIOCHT NAOFA: A Scripture Quotation

Bless the Lord, O my soul, you set the beams of your chambers
on the waters, you make the clouds your chariot, you ride on the
wings of the wind, you make the winds your messengers, fire and
flame your ministers, you cause the grass to grow, to bring forth
food from the earth and wine to gladden the human heart and
oil to make the face shine.
Psalm 104

✺ ❊ ✺ ❊ ✺ ❊ ✺ ❊ ✺ ❊ ✺ ❊ ✺ ❊ ✺ ❊ ✺ ❊ ✺ ❊ ✺ ❊ ✺

AN PAIDIR CHIÚIN: Silent Prayer

The timing here will vary according to your schedule. Ring a
bell or a chime as you imaginatively step into your own oarless
currach of trust and hope. Let your busy mind float adrift for
a spell. Ring the bell to herald your arrival at the shore of the
day's destiny.

AN PAIDIR PHEARSANTA: Personal Prayer

Whatever intuition or memo came to you during your *paidir chiúin*, commit now to prayer – either aloud or in your heart; honouring your own moment of need, then the needs of someone close or indeed not so dear to you and, finally, extending that blessing out to the universe, particularly those war-torn lands and starving peoples.

DÁN DÉ AN LÁ: Sacred Verse of the Day

Now I lay me down to sleep,
I pray my lord my soul to keep,
In the morning, when I awake
Please teach me the path of life to take.
Grace Bridges, 1932

BEANNACHT DEIRIGH: Final Blessing

St Nicholas, patron of children, we pray this night for your protection for the children of the world, the next generation. May they know that we tried as best we could to raise them in goodness and we pray, in harmony with the heart chakra, for pardon for the times we fell short.

Green is the colour of the Heart chakra – Anahata – a colour associated with envy. May our hearts enlarge this night so that we may wake courageous and fearless for the day ahead. May I celebrate the gifts of others and have no desire to possess them.

MÚCHADH AN CHOINNEALL:
Extinguish Your Earthly Candle
Knowing that, although you are blowing out your *coinneal domhanda* (earthly flame), your blessed angelic light continues to flicker for you this night.

DÉ hAOINE: Friday

Friday is the holiest day of the week in Islamic tradition.

Christ (the Divine/Human one who died on his day by tradition/Mother Goddess)

Vishuddhi – Lakshmi – Throat chakra

Maidin: Morning

AN CHOINEALL BEO: The Living Candle
Light your candle, and prepare for the ritual that follows.

❋❁❋❁❋❁❋❁❋❁❋❁❋❁❋❁❋❁❋❁❋❁❋❁❋❁❋

AN GLAOCH CHUN URNAÍ: Opening Call to Prayer
Lord, open my lips and my mouth will declare your praise.
(Psalm 51)

Repeat this three times and make a blessing on your lips.

❋❁❋❁❋❁❋❁❋❁❋❁❋❁❋❁❋❁❋❁❋❁❋❁❋❁❋

SLIOCHT NAOFA: A Scripture Quotation
*Creator of the universe, grant me the ability to be alone. May
it be my custom to go outdoors each day, among the trees and
grasses, among all growing things there, to be alone and enter
into prayer. There, may I express all that is in my heart, talking
with You, to whom I belong. And may all grasses, trees, and
plants awake at my coming. Send the power of their life into my
prayer, making whole my heart and my speech through the life
and spirit of growing things, made whole by their transcendent
Source. O that they would enter into my prayer! Then would
I fully open my heart in prayer, supplication and holy speech;
then, O God, would I pour out the words of my heart before
Your presence.*
Reb Nachman of Bratslav

AN PAIDIR CHIÚIN: Silent Prayer

The timing here will vary according to your schedule. Ring a bell or a chime as you imaginatively step into your own oarless *currach* of trust and hope. Let your busy mind float adrift for a spell. Ring the bell to herald your arrival at the shore of the day's destiny.

AN PAIDIR PHEARSANTA: Personal Prayer

Whatever intuition or memo came to you during your *paidir chiúin*, commit now to prayer – either aloud or in your heart; honouring your own moment of need, then the needs of someone close or indeed not so dear to you and, finally, extending that blessing out to the universe, particularly those war-torn lands and starving peoples.

DÁN DÉ AN LÁ: Sacred Verse of the Day

If I can stop one Heart from breaking
I shall not live in vain
If I can ease one Life the Aching
Or cool one Pain
Or help one fainting Robin
Unto his Nest again
I shall not live in vain.
Emily Dickinson

BEANNACHT DEIRIGH: Final Blessing

From Islam we are told *'when the call is made for prayer on Friday, hurry toward the remembrance of God'*. May the Human/ Divine Christ accompany us in this commemoration today, to see myself as a good person but most of allow myself to live fully with all my faults, beauty and frailties.

Great mother, Lakshmi, great goddess of beauty, prosperity and wealth, help me to detect the innate beauty around me, in those I meet today and in my surroundings. Let me not be deluded by false wealth but seek the true riches which the Divine freely pours out on the soul. May I keep in mind, this day the adage of the 6th century BCE Chinese sage, Confucius, who believed: *'everything has beauty in it but not everyone can see it'*.

From the throat chakra – Vishuddhi – we speak our truth with confidence and gentleness.

May I never break a promise or go back on a word but always speak the veracity of my story.

MÚCHADH AN CHOINNEALL:
Extinguish Your Earthly Candle

Knowing that, although you are blowing out your *coinneal domhanda* (earthly flame), your blessed angelic light continues to flicker for you today.

TRÁTHNÓNA: *Evening*

AN CHOINEALL BEO: The Living Candle

Light your candle, and prepare for the ritual that follows.

❋◦❋◦❋◦❋◦❋◦❋◦❋◦❋◦❋◦❋◦❋◦❋◦❋◦❋◦❋

AN GLAOCH CHUN URNAÍ: Opening Call to Prayer

O God, come to my aid, O Lord make haste to help me.
(Psalm 70)

Make the sign of the cross as you say this.

❋◦❋◦❋◦❋◦❋◦❋◦❋◦❋◦❋◦❋◦❋◦❋◦❋◦❋◦❋

SLIOCHT NAOFA: A Scripture Quotation

So do not worry about tomorrow for tomorrow will bring worries of its own. Today's trouble is enough for today.
Matthew 6:34

❋◦❋◦❋◦❋◦❋◦❋◦❋◦❋◦❋◦❋◦❋◦❋◦❋◦❋◦❋

AN PAIDIR CHIÚIN: Silent Prayer

The timing here will vary according to your schedule. Ring a bell or a chime as you imaginatively step into your own oarless *currach* of trust and hope. Let your busy mind float adrift for a spell. Ring the bell to herald your arrival at the shore of the day's destiny.

AN PAIDIR PHEARSANTA: Personal Prayer

Whatever intuition or memo came to you during your *paidir chiúin*, commit now to prayer – either aloud or in your heart; honouring your own moment of need, then the needs of someone close or indeed not so dear to you and, finally, extending that blessing out to the universe, particularly those war-torn lands and starving peoples.

❈❈❈❈❈❈❈❈❈❈❈❈❈❈❈❈❈❈

DÁN DÉ AN LÁ – Sacred Verse of the Day

Stay with us, for it is evening and the day is now far spent.
Luke 24:29

❈❈❈❈❈❈❈❈❈❈❈❈❈❈❈❈❈❈

BEANNACHT DEIRIGH: Final Blessing

When Friday prayer is finished, '*disperse through the land and seek God's grace, and remember God greatly so that you may be successful*'. (Qu'ran, Surah Al-Jumu'ah (62), Ayahs 9-10)

Great Divine Feminine Lakshmi, I invite you to visit my home this night. Your bird is the owl, wise and discerning, seeing clearly through the darkness. Guide me now not to be blinded by material wealth but bring me safe throughout the night to rise and see the bright path before me in the morning.

The heart chakra – Vishuddhi – shelters our speech and our hearing. This evening, may my hearing be sharpened in my dreams to listen and to hear the sound of your voice, my creator and shepherd of my soul. Peter, fisherman and apostle to Jesus Christ, sums up the thriving heart chakra thus: *'Always be ready to make your defence … an accounting for the hope that is in you; but do it gently, and with respect, with a clear conscience.'* (1 Peter 3: 15–16)

MÚCHADH AN CHOINNEALL:
Extinguish Your Earthly Candle
Knowing that, although you are blowing out your *coinneal domhanda* (earthly flame), your blessed angelic light continues to flicker for you this night.

DÉ SATHAIRN: Saturday

Mary (mother of God, the Divine Feminine)

Ajna – Lord Shani – Third Eye/Ear

Maidin: Morning

AN CHOINEALL BEO: The Living Candle

Light your candle, and prepare for the ritual that follows.

AN GLAOCH CHUN URNAÍ:

Opening Call to Prayer

Lord, open my lips and my mouth will declare your praise.
(Psalm 51)

Repeat this three times and make a blessing on your lips.

SLIOCHT NAOFA: A Scripture Quotation

May I bring sustenance, gratitude and awakening
Enduring like the earth and sky
Until all beings are freed from sorrow
And all are awakened.
Shantideva, Indian Buddhist sage 700 CE

AN PAIDIR CHIÚIN: Silent Prayer

The timing here will vary according to your schedule. Ring a bell or a chime as you imaginatively step into your own oarless *currach* of trust and hope. Let your busy mind float adrift for a spell. Ring the bell to herald your arrival at the shore of the day's destiny.

AN PAIDIR PHEARSANTA: Personal Prayer

Whatever intuition or memo came to you during your *paidir chiúin*, commit now to prayer – either aloud or in your heart; honouring your own moment of need, then the needs of someone close or indeed not so dear to you and, finally, extending that blessing out to the universe, particularly those war-torn lands and starving peoples.

※✴※✴※✴※✴※✴※✴※✴※✴※✴※✴※✴※✴※✴※

DÁN DÉ AN LÁ: Sacred Verse of the Day

Drive away the darkness that surrounds us.
Shed around us the mantle of your light.
Help us to know your will,
And give us the courage to do it.
Mark Patrick Hederman
– Icon Chapel Daily Prayer, Glenstal Abbey

BEANNACHT DEIRIGH: Final Blessing

In Irish, you are Muire. In Eastern Christianity you are *Theotokos,* which means the God-bearer. May I be the bearer of the sacred, the Divine in myself and for others in my work, in my family and friends.

Lord Shani, god of justice, may my words, thoughts and actions reflect your dedication to fairness and justice. Son of tomorrow's God, Surya, we call on you to prepare our way justly to celebrate the end of this week.

Intuition and imagination are the hallmarks of the Third Eye/Ear chakra – Ajna – may these two realms of existence live in abundance in me today.

MÚCHADH AN CHOINNEALL:

Extinguish Your Earthly Candle

Knowing that, although you are blowing out your *coinneal domhanda* (earthly flame), your blessed angelic light continues to flicker for you this day.

TRÁTHNÓNA: *Evening*

AN CHOINEALL BEO: The Living Candle
Light your candle, and prepare for the ritual that follows.

AN GLAOCH CHUN URNAÍ: Opening Call to Prayer
O God, come to my aid, O Lord make haste to help me.
(Psalm 70)

Make the sign of the cross as you say this.

SLIOCHT NAOFA: A Scripture Quotation
Great Mystery teach me how to trust
my heart,
my mind,
my intuition,
my inner knowing,
the senses of my body,
the blessings of my spirit.
Teach me to trust these things so that
I may enter my Sacred Space
and love beyond my fear.
Lakota, Native American prayer

AN PAIDIR CHIÚIN: Silent Prayer

The timing here will vary according to your schedule. Ring a bell or a chime as you imaginatively step into your own oarless *currach* of trust and hope. Let your busy mind float adrift for a spell. Ring the bell to herald your arrival at the shore of the day's destiny.

AN PAIDIR PHEARSANTA: Personal Prayer

Whatever intuition or memo came to you during your *paidir chiúin*, commit now to prayer – either aloud or in your heart; honouring your own moment of need, then the needs of someone close or indeed not so dear to you and, finally, extending that blessing out to the universe, particularly those war-torn lands and starving peoples.

❋❋❋❋❋❋❋❋❋❋❋❋❋❋❋❋❋❋

DÁN DÉ AN LÁ: Sacred Verse of the Day

Lord, behold our family here assembled.
We thank you for this place in which we dwell,
for the love that unites us,
for the peace accorded to us this day,
for the hope with which we expect the morrow;
for the health, the work,
the food and the bright skies
that make our lives delightful;
for our friends in all parts of the earth. Amen.
Robert Louis Stevenson, excerpt from 'Success', Prayers written at Vailima

BEANNACHT DEIRIGH: Final Blessing

Hail Mary, full of grace … Holy Mary, Mother of God, pray for us now and at the hour of our death.

May the blessings of Lord Shani rain down upon me all the days of my life. You preside over longevity and old age, make us know the shortness of our days so that we may cherish each moment and not waste it on useless worry and anxiety, this night.

May our dreams this night through the grace of the third eye/ ear chakra – ajna – feed our imaginings, our visions and our inventiveness. In the morning we will rise sustained in this power.

May the divine feminine be with us this evening and through the night.

MÚCHADH AN CHOINNEALL:
Extinguish Your Earthly Candle

Knowing that, although you are blowing out your *coinneal domhanda* (earthly flame), your blessed angelic light continues to flicker for you this night.

DÉ DOMHNAIGH: Sunday

God the Creator of new Life and Resurrection

Sahasrara – Lord Surya – Crown Chakra –

Maidin: Morning

AN CHOINEALL BEO: The Living Candle
Light your candle, and prepare for the ritual that follows.

AN GLAOCH CHUN URNAÍ: Opening Call to Prayer
Lord, open my lips and my mouth will declare your praise.
(Psalm 51)

Repeat this three times and make a blessing on your lips.

SLIOCHT NAOFA: A Scripture Quotation

Fore-run by mind are mental states
Ruled by mind, made of mind.
If you speak or act with corrupt mind
Sorrow follows you, as the wheel the foot of the ox.

Fore-run by mind are mental states
Ruled by mind, made of mind.
If you speak or act with clear mind
Happiness follows you, like a shadow that does not depart.
Buddhism Dhammapada, The Sayings of the Buddha
(1: 1-2)

※＊※＊※＊※＊※＊※＊※＊※＊※＊※＊※＊※＊※＊※

AN PAIDIR CHIÚIN: Silent Prayer

The timing here will vary according to your schedule. Ring a bell or a chime as you imaginatively step into your own oarless *currach* of trust and hope. Let your busy mind float adrift for a spell. Ring the bell to herald your arrival at the shore of the day's destiny.

AN PAIDIR PHEARSANTA: Personal Prayer

Whatever intuition or memo came to you during your *paidir chiúin*, commit now to prayer – either aloud or in your heart; honouring your own moment of need, then the needs

of someone close or indeed not so dear to you and, finally, extending that blessing out to the universe, particularly those war-torn lands and starving peoples.

DÁN DÉ AN LÁ: Sacred Verse of the Day

Allah says, 'Take one step towards me, I will take ten steps towards you. Walk towards me, I will run towards you.'
Hadith Qudse

BEANNACHT DEIRIGH: Final Blessing

This is the legendary day when God rested after all the noble labour of creation. At rest in Irish is 'fé shuan/fé shuaimhneas', which implies being under a spell of peace and serenity.

May I know that real rest value today, which is not one of laziness or inertia. I will treasure this day as I strive to replenish my strength and sacred connection to embrace the week ahead.

Lord Surya, you are the supreme deity, source of all creation and bearer of light. As you travel the earth daily in your chariot of gold, bless us this day, which honours your supreme soul that brings light to the cosmos.

Sahasrara of the thousand multicoloured lotus, and seat and throne of God, you are the source of all other chakras. You will liberate me into your realm of pure consciousness and free me from the self-centred ego.

May the waves of my brain, through your strength, radiate outward to unite my soul with God.

❉∗❉∗❉∗❉∗❉∗❉∗❉∗❉∗❉∗❉∗❉∗❉∗❉∗❉∗❉∗❉

MÚCHADH AN CHOINNEALL:
Extinguish Your Earthly Candle
Knowing that, although you are blowing out your *coinneal domhanda* (earthly flame), your blessed angelic light continues to flicker for you this day.

TRÁTHNÓNA: Evening

AN CHOINEALL BEO: The Living Candle
Light your candle, and prepare for the ritual that follows.

❉∗❉∗❉∗❉∗❉∗❉∗❉∗❉∗❉∗❉∗❉∗❉∗❉∗❉∗❉∗❉

AN GLAOCH CHUN URNAÍ: Opening Call to Prayer
O God, come to my aid, O Lord make haste to help me.
(Psalm 70)

Make the sign of the cross as you say this.

✹❅✹❅✹❅✹❅✹❅✹❅✹❅✹❅✹❅✹❅✹❅✹❅✹❅✹❅✹❅✹

SLIOCHT NAOFA: A Scripture Quotation

In everything do to others as you would have them do to you; for this is the law and the prophets.
Matthew 7:12

✹❅✹❅✹❅✹❅✹❅✹❅✹❅✹❅✹❅✹❅✹❅✹❅✹❅✹❅✹❅✹

AN PAIDIR CHIÚIN: Silent Prayer

The timing here will vary according to your schedule. Ring a bell or a chime as you imaginatively step into your own oarless *currach* of trust and hope. Let your busy mind float adrift for a spell. Ring the bell to herald your arrival at the shore of the day's destiny.

AN PAIDIR PHEARSANTA: Personal Prayer

Whatever intuition or memo came to you during your *paidir chiúin*, commit now to prayer – either aloud or in your heart; honouring your own moment of need, then the needs of someone close or indeed not so dear to you and, finally, extending that blessing out to the universe, particularly those war-torn lands and starving peoples.

✹❅✹❅✹❅✹❅✹❅✹❅✹❅✹❅✹❅✹❅✹❅✹❅✹❅✹❅✹❅✹

DÁN DÉ AN LÁ:
Sacred Verse of the Day

Be thou a bright flame before me
Be thou a guiding star above me
Be thou a smooth path beneath me
Be thou a kindly shepherd behind me
Today, tonight and forever.

St Colmcille, patron saint of Ireland

BEANNACHT DEIRIGH: Final Blessing

Now that we have come to the close of our week, I look back in great gratitude to the Creator who gave me this time. Thank you for a miniature, earthly experience of Resurrection. I know that the dawn tomorrow will not just be the beginning of the rest of my life, but of new being in time and probability.

Lord Surya, God of tomorrow's sun who can be seen with human eyes, let me know your love. Instil in me your knowledge, clarity and power to drive away all the darkness that may be lurking this night and in the week ahead.

Ending this weekly cycle, I appeal to the crowning glory – Sahasrara – to align the most important essence of my being – my spirituality. From this energy centre arises the power of true communion with myself, with others and ultimately with the Divine. Amen – so be it.

MÚCHADH AN CHOINNEALL:
Extinguish Your Earthly Candle

Knowing that, although you are blowing out your *coinneal domhanda* (earthly flame), your blessed angelic light continues to flicker for you this night.

BEANNACHT ROIMH AGUS AG DEIRE BÉILÍ: Grace Before and After Meals

A blessing bestowed upon food before and after eating is called a Grace. When we wake to the marvel of the food before us and of which we have just cherished, we become aware of at least four insights into the wonder, the grace, of it all.

- The companionship, the friendship we share.

- The awe of the universe that gifted us with this nourishment.

- The care and gifts of the hands that delivered it and that prepared it.

- Most importantly, the keen awareness of the harrowing reality of world hunger and greed.

Pope Francis urges everyone '*to return to this beautiful and meaningful custom*' of blessing food before and after meals. May each morsel and each drop we partake of be a prayer.

A word here on the lone meal table. Often our understanding of a blessing with food can be confined to socialised, shared mealtimes. But if you choose to live on your own, as I do, a blessing ritual creates new understandings for the solitary meal. Food is even more precious and savoured; every morsel is a prayer precisely because we have time to ponder and really taste the good of it. Every kitchen table, round or square, seating one, two or more people, can become a temple of holiness.

DO BHEANNACHT BIA:
Your Own Grace Ritual

Begin by holding hands with table companions and bread breakers. If you are on your own, raise your hands upwards as you give thanks for 'the fruit of the vine and the work of human hands'. Commit the food before you to a deity of your choice. Annapurna is the popular Hindu food goddess. In Christianity, the patron saint of cooks is a third-century Roman martyr named Lawrence because a rather gruesome legend tells us that when he was being roasted over a gridiron, he addressed his torturers thus: '*I am cooked on this side, turn me around now and eat*'.

Give thanks first and foremost. Address the universe that provided this food and the human hands that prepared it – the sky, sea, and earth and the caring workers behind the offering.

A blessing now for each person gathered at the table that we may eat in moderation and in a manner that enhances our love and compassion for our own physical and spiritual selves and for others.

Finally, remember all those without food, either physically or spiritually, at this time.

Below are a couple of prayers that you can use, there are more in the Last Word section of additional prayers.

As we begin our meal with grace, let us become aware that this food is the gift of the entire universe, the earth, the sky and much hard work, the work of all the strangers whose hands prepared it. We give thanks for the privilege of wealth and health that enables us to feast and celebrate.

❋❋❋❋❋❋❋❋❋❋❋❋❋❋❋❋

Islamic Prayer
O God our Lord, send a table down to us from Heaven above.

Make the day of its coming like a festival for us, for you are the best provider.

Qu'ran

We end our meal with grace, for the joy and nourishment of food and wine that slowed time away from the world, to come into presence with each other and sense the subtle lives behind our faces. The different colours of our voices, the circle of love that unites us. We pray the wise spirit who keeps us – to change the structures that make and keep others hungry.

And that after such grace, we might now go forth and impart dignity, compassion and love wherever we partake.

May it be pleasing to Allah.

Traditional Islamic grace

DÉAN É TÚ FÉIN : A DIY of Planning and Preparation for any Ritual

You now have been through the tools to and are primed to begin the self-assembly of ritual. As you grow more confident in your own practices, you may begin to gather prayers and poems that speak to you and ones you keep aside for possible specific intentions. Throughout your journey with prayer ritual, there will come times when you wish to dedicate a ritual to a special intention, such as loneliness, illness or gratitude. In this section I have outlined a DIY of how to plan one of these rituals, to guide you through these sessions. Prepare to enter your altar sanctuary or your place of quiet shelter where you can feel secure and safe.

- Light a candle of focus that will inspire you to maintain your own steady flame of composure during your heart ritual and of course to remember you to your heavenly light.

- Search out whatever body position that is the calmest way in which you can be open to the voice of the Spirit.

- This is the crucial moment. Bring to the altar and its steady candle flame, the heart matter that is crowding you out at this moment. Is it fear anxiety, addiction grief, loss, ageing, death and dying, love questions, self-love, forgiveness or indeed gratitude for all that is?

- Take your notebook and pen and write as humbly and as honestly as you can how you are feeling about the concerns you have. (Incidentally, I often use a pencil to write, which has an eraser at the top. Sometimes, you may want to erase your writing or rephrase your words.)

- Now go to the ritual below that matches your needs and read aloud the prayers and reflections there. Stretch out your hand and hold it gently but firmly and when you call it by name, find the prayer here that fits.

- Invite in first your heart with its never-sleeping, single rhythm drumbeat. Feel the pulsation as you open your ears through positioning your right hand in the centre of your chest. Know that your heart is calming down now and returning to when it was in your mother's womb throbbing at her heart rate and yours with hers.

- Close or half close your eyes. To drop your eyelids is to give edge to your ears and awaken to the tenderness of sound around you. The ear is always wondering and in wonder at the mystery, the otherness, of everything outside of us.

- To close your heart ritual, return to your notepad and jot down any intuitions or shifts in perspectives that may have occurred during this time.

- Stand now and as you turn towards your life, make a prayerful sign of protection around yourself. In ancient Irish tradition, this safeguard was called a *sciathlúireach* or breastplate – a personal armour that shields from darkness. Mine is making the Sign of the Cross on my forehead, ears, eyes, lips, and heart.

- Extinguish your candle in gratitude. Watch the residual smoke rise and disappear finally as if it were transporting your wants and wishes up to the Divine Other.

MACHNAMH MAIDINE: Morning Meditation

My early, first-waking morning ritual of thanksgiving to God was greatly enhanced and enriched when I learned a Jewish morning prayer. A greater fullness of presence of the divine has been the unexpected beautiful gift that other religions have brought to my door. At the very moment of waking in bed, the

Modeh Ani prayer of thanksgiving is offered: gratitude to that Spirit for restoring the soul to new life and fresh possibility for this original day.

❊﹡❊﹡❊﹡❊﹡❊﹡❊﹡❊﹡❊﹡❊﹡❊﹡❊﹡❊﹡❊

Modah/modeh ani lefanekha
melekh ḥai vekayam
sheheḥezarta bi nishmati
b'ḥemlah, rabah emunatekha.

I give thanks before you,
Spirit, living and eternal,
for You have returned within me my soul with compassion;
abundant is Your faithfulness!

❊﹡❊﹡❊﹡❊﹡❊﹡❊﹡❊﹡❊﹡❊﹡❊﹡❊﹡❊﹡❊

Before my feet hit the ground, I add my own version of a fragment of this Hebrew soul prayer in Irish.

❊﹡❊﹡❊﹡❊﹡❊﹡❊﹡❊﹡❊﹡❊﹡❊﹡❊﹡❊﹡❊

A Dhia bheo, buiochas leat a thug m'anam slán sabhailte I gcaitheamh na hoíche, flúirseach de thrua ionamsa.

Almighty God, Creator: the morning is yours, rising into fullness. The summer is yours, dipping into autumn. Eternity is yours, dipping into time. The vibrant grasses, the scent of flowers, the lichen on the rocks, the tang of seaweed. All is yours. Gladly we live in this garden of your creating.
Celtic Prayer

A Íosa a Mhic Dé, a bhí ciúin os comhair Pioláit; ná leig dúinn ár dteanga do luasgadh gan smaoineamh ar cad atá againn le rá agus cionnus é do rádh.

Jesus, son of God, you were silent before Pilate; do not allow our tongues to wag without thinking about what we have to say and how best to say it.
Irish Traditional, County Louth

O Great Spirit, help me always to speak the truth quietly, to listen with an open mind when others speak, and to remember the peace that may be found in silence.
Native American, Cherokee Prayer

Yours is the light that breaks from the dark … yours is the gift that still is gain when everything is a loss, and the life that flows through the caverns of death. Yours is the heaven that lives in the common dust, and you are there for me. You are there for all.
Rabindranath Tagore

PAIDIR TRÁTHNÓNA CRÍOCHNAITHEACH: Evening Prayer

My night-time is both a blessing and a sometimes scourge. A *beannacht* (blessing) because, most days, I like to shut the door on the world of the day, say my evening prayers, read over a nutritious solitary meal and, of course, the glass of Merlot! A curse, because although I love retiring into the dreamworld, getting there – falling asleep – does not always come easily. The only fallings we welcome are in love and asleep; any other thought of tumbling petrifies us. But both love and sleep can resist the fall.

At these times, though, my consolation is knowing that I am not alone. I remember that God is an insomniac! Like your two ears, always awake and alert to our every move. Let me qualify this insomnia claim. It is a state that we, humans, dread. We see the word and shudder. Hours of tossing and turning in the bed, nocturnal relentless anxieties leave us all at one time or another even more tired and weary. No one wants or choose this harrowing visitor. However, God doesn't nap – and never dozes off, the Psalmist assures us: *'May God sleep not, your guard. No, God sleeps not nor slumbers',* (Psalm 120) The prophet Isaiah endorses this: God does not *'faint or grow weary'.* (Isaiah 40:28)

When the day is done and night-time descends, our inner world comes alive to the outer darkness. A complexity of emotions haunt us. Particularly at eventide, we long for protection and ease. You take a review of the day you have just lived and try to make sense of it all. You can ask yourself; how did I spend this day? What good – or indeed the opposite – did I do today for myself and for others? What have I to be truly grateful for? Where did I fail or fall short?

When I reassess my day during my evening prayer, I am inspired by the nocturnal ritual of Teresa of Ávila. Every night, she held each being she encountered that day in her heart, shaping hers like theirs and theirs like hers. My last gesture of the day often is to make the shape of a heart with my two hands, thumbs meeting and facing downward, index fingers curled and joining together.

Our ancestors turned towards the awesome night sky to assure themselves of the presence of the Divine through the moon and stars. This time for prayer is in a different scale of *raga,* as the Hindu tradition would name it.

Anxiety when you wake in the night – staring into the darkness – is a nightmare in reality. There must be something about being horizontal that amplifies worry and stress.

Better to rise and pray a little than shiver it out. Physical darkness shadows the temple of our fears. When my vulnerabilities and sense of loneliness trip me up at night, here is a prayer that calms me and eventually accompanies me into sleep. Read – aloud if you can – this night prayer here and trust in them to bring you home to yourself each night and to inveigle you into the realm of deep sleep and dreams.

＊＊＊＊＊＊＊＊＊＊＊＊＊＊＊＊＊＊＊＊＊＊＊＊＊

O Great Spirit, help me always to speak the truth quietly, to listen with an open mind when others speak, and to remember the peace that may be found in silence.
Native American, Cherokee Prayer

＊＊＊＊＊＊＊＊＊＊＊＊＊＊＊＊＊＊＊＊＊＊＊＊＊

PAIDREACHA AM AISLING:
Holy Dream Time

Retiring at night is a ritual I now welcome because I am always curious and excited about where my dreams will carry me. I remember the adventures so vividly. In the early morning, I dwell for a few minutes in a liminal world. I am still in my dream domain yet about to face reality, my real, physical belonging to this earth; sometimes disappointed at the fading into the mists of my marvellous dream world, sometimes comforted and consoled to be back safe and sound from some nightmarish scenario.

Many, many times, I was so convinced that my dream-time was actual reality that I would try to persuade the one nearest to me of its validity. Two particular mornings come to mind. Both were when I slept beside my then husband, Mícheál. Once, we were staying in a hotel near Cashel, County Tipperary. I can still recall the manager coming into our bedroom and standing at the end of the bed. 'We have run out of bread in the hotel,' he said. 'I am so sorry, but you should drive into the town and get breakfast there.'

'That was strange, wasn't it, Mick?' I said on waking.

'What was?'

'You don't remember?' I asked incredulously. Very reluctantly and after much coaxing on his part, I accompanied him to the restaurant where baskets full of brown bread and toast adorned every table!

Another morning, we were staying overnight in my family home in Caherconlish in County Limerick, and I had what transpired to be a prophetic dream. A choir of twelve monks appeared in the room and were standing, chanting before a great mirror which was on the door of the wardrobe. I woke Mick up excitedly and said, 'Look at the monks.' But they had disappeared from sight! Just six months after this reverie, the monks of Glenstal Abbey entered our lives. But my vision did get one detail wrong! The fantasy monks were dressed in brown habits whereas the Benedictines in the nearby monastery wear black!

MANTRAS: Mantras for a peaceful mind before sleep

Sometimes, we do not have the time, the patience, the possibility of entering a timeless prayer capsule. So, memorise a few of these 'mantras' and you will never be alone again.

A mantra is an 'instrument', a tool that saves the meditating psyche. A mantra moulds the rough clay of thought into a precious pearl nudging us on. The advice of St Benedict in his *Rule* is: '*It is not in saying a great deal that we shall be heard …*

our prayer, therefore, ought to be short and pure ... let prayer be very short ... ' (Chapter 20)

The Buddhist tradition names their terse verses *gathas*, usually recited in harmony with the breathing rhythm of the worshipper. The same-sounding word in Irish is *geata*, which means 'gate'. These pithy sacred verses are simply portals into the company – divine, cosmic or both – of one's heart's desire.

❊❊❊❊❊❊❊❊❊❊❊❊❊❊❊❊❊❊❊❊❊❊

'Stay with us, for it is evening and the day is now far spent.'
Luke 24:29

❊❊❊❊❊❊❊❊❊❊❊❊❊❊❊❊❊❊❊❊❊❊

'O resplendent Night, may you lead us sinless to dawn, from dawn to day, and from day back to you!'
Atharva Veda XIX

❊❊❊❊❊❊❊❊❊❊❊❊❊❊❊❊❊❊❊❊❊❊

May all I say and all I think
Be in harmony with thee,
God within me, God beyond me,
Maker of trees.
Native American, Chinook Prayer

DEASGHÁTHA LE HAGAIDH CÚRSAÍ CROÍ: Rituals for Heart Matters

There are so many faces to love and yet do we really know what it is? Even the renowned psychiatrist and psychologist, Carl Jung, failed to define it in words: '*I falter before the task of finding the language that might adequately express the incalculable paradoxes of love.*' He claimed St Paul came closest in that inspired passage of his to the people of Corinth written in the first century.

※⚹※⚹※⚹※⚹※⚹※⚹※⚹※⚹※⚹※⚹※⚹※⚹※⚹※⚹※⚹※

If I speak in the tongues of men and of angels, but have not love, I am only a resounding gong or a clanging cymbal. If I have the gift of prophecy and can fathom all mysteries and all knowledge, and if I have a faith that can move mountains, but have not love, I am nothing.

1 Corinthians 13: 1

※⚹※⚹※⚹※⚹※⚹※⚹※⚹※⚹※⚹※⚹※⚹※⚹※⚹※⚹※⚹※

I hear this passage all the time during marriage ceremonies in my ministry and, every time, some new insight comes to ambush me. Just two days ago at a wedding in Cork, the moral of the Corinthian letter was that now is the time to leave our childlike behaviour behind, to challenge our world face to face, realising its transience but also embracing it with faith, hope and love. '*The greatest of these is love.*' (1 Corinthians 13)

✻❀✻❀✻❀✻❀✻❀✻❀✻❀✻❀✻❀✻❀✻❀✻❀✻❀✻

Come, my joy, my Love, my Heart:
Such a Joy, as none can move:
Such a Love, as none can part:
Such a Heart, as joys in love.
George Herbert, excerpt from 'The Temple'

✻❀✻❀✻❀✻❀✻❀✻❀✻❀✻❀✻❀✻❀✻❀✻❀✻❀✻

Arise, my love, my fair one, and come away. For now the winter is past, the rain is over and gone. The flowers appear on the earth; the time of singing has come and the voice of the turtledove is heard in our land.
Song of Songs 2:10-12

✻❀✻❀✻❀✻❀✻❀✻❀✻❀✻❀✻❀✻❀✻❀✻❀✻❀✻

FÉIN-GHRÁ: Self-Love

The term 'Golden Rule' appears out of nowhere but its moral is very clear: 'Treat others as you would wish to be treated'; do not do anything to another that you would not have done unto you. This ethical belief is held by *all* the major religions. However, we can turn the tables here to begin at home. Love yourself as you love others.

The concept of love of oneself is only possible if we extend our love outwards as well. As Scripture resiliently advises: '*Love your neighbour as yourself.*' This loaded phrase first appears in the Old Testament, Book of Leviticus, only to be repeated nine times in the New Testament. The measure that we appreciate ourselves is only to be matched by the ration of love we can bestow upon others. If there is no self-love, there is no another-love. If there is no caring for self, there is no caring for others. Surely the current proliferation of self-help resources is in direct response to the neglect of the second half of this Scriptural proverb 'as yourself'.

Now for our Golden Rule prayer moment, recognise the startling truth of the Golden Rule: Do unto others as you would have them do unto you as you enter your sacred space. Close your eyes. If, in the morning, consider the day before you and make a resolution to only treat others this day as you would wish to be treated yourself. If, in the evening, scan your day and in humility and self-forgiveness, surrender yourself to an honest appraisal of how you treated others *and* yourself.

Take a moment before you open your heart to the following poems. First begin with a hand gesture, that of palms together as in namaste greeting. Then gently move your right hand to your left shoulder and your left to the right.

❀❀❀❀❀❀❀❀❀❀❀❀❀❀❀❀❀❀❀❀❀❀❀

You never enjoy the world aright,
Till the sea itself floweth in your veins,
Till you are clothed with the heavens,
And crowned with the stars;
And perceive yourself to be the sole heir
Of the whole world.
Thomas Traherne, *Centuries of Meditation*

❀❀❀❀❀❀❀❀❀❀❀❀❀❀❀❀❀❀❀❀❀❀❀

Bring your Golden Rule meditation to a close by reading the following narrative on the greatest power of love, which is prayer.

Strange how a poem – or prayer – comes to our door just at the right time to waylay our lives and transform us in ways beyond our imagination. This is how George Herbert's poem 'Love' birthed an entire new life of prayer for Simone Weil, the French philosopher. She recalls the experience in her book *Waiting on God*.

❋❋❋❋❋❋❋❋❋❋❋❋❋❋❋❋❋❋❋❋❋

I heard by chance … the poem called 'Love'. I learned it by heart … I used to think I was merely reciting it as a beautiful poem, but without my knowing it the recitation had the virtue of a PRAYER … Until last September I had never once prayed to God in all my life.

❋❋❋❋❋❋❋❋❋❋❋❋❋❋❋❋❋❋❋❋❋

This poem is an entire poetic synopsis of interfaith spirituality. For George Herbert, the Divine Love is waiting with apron on and pots and pans ready to serve everyone equally and unreservedly.

Here is a lyrical reading of many scriptural passages in which Herbert was very well-versed. You will hear echoes of 'The Prodigal Son', Job's humility and reticence before the Divine and God's response to that, and all the analogies to banqueting, feasting and service that are dotted throughout. I love the image of the 'smiling' servant reminding us of who created our ordinary/extraordinary being, our common/ uncommon beauty through which we see and hear. At the end of the day, the only proper ritual to the call of prayer is to sit and eat.

Love bade me welcome, yet my soul drew back,
Guilty of dust and sin.
But quick-eyed Love, observing me grow slack
From my first entrance in,
Drew nearer to me, sweetly questioning
If I lack'd anything.
'A guest,' I answer'd, 'worthy to be here.'
Love said, 'You shall be he.'
'I, the unkind, ungrateful? Ah, my dear,
I cannot look on Thee.'
Love took my hand and smiling did reply,
'Who made the eyes but I?'
'Truth, Lord, but I have marr'd them: let my shame
Go where it doth deserve.'
'And know you not,' says Love, 'who bore the blame?'
'My dear, then I will serve.'
'You must sit down,' says Love, 'and taste my meat.'
So I did sit and eat.
George Herbert 'LOVE III'

SGARÚINT NA gCOMPÁNAIGH:
When Love Runs Dry

In the void between two people in love, Spirit steps in to bind four hands. Marriage or living together seals this but sometimes only for a while. Often, the invisible shared cloak woven together in this space between frays. Threads break and rend until the whole fabric is torn, no longer fit for providing a sure shelter. Four hands become two again. To sever this hand-fasting, cries out for – a rite of passage – to move on as best you can.

When our twenty-year love teetered, my husband and I prayed together. Not to mend or patch the tears with empty promises but for strength to face out in different directions to the future. The prospect of a loveless, monotonous lukewarm rapport haunted us. Better to part now and embrace a future life vibrating with possibility and self-growth than remain in a hellish routine.

Although the pathway was rough, we did create a shared trail of friendship through those years apart, until Micheál's death in 2018. Our nameless, albeit unspoken, rituals of reconciliation were both small healers and gentle mementos of a one-time love. He, although weak at the time of his passing, was present at my ordination in London in 2017. I sang at his wedding some weeks later. Every love is a blessing no matter its duration.

Lord Alfred Tennyson's oft quoted quatrain is true.

I hold it true what'ere befall
I felt it when I sorrow most
'Tis Better to have loved and lost
Than never to have loved at all.
Alfred, Lord Tennyson, Verse XXVII, 'In Memoriam'

To be the conduit of reconciliation rituals was a desire within me from my own experience. No marriage is a failure; there were the happy moments that were blessings from God. The church celebrates the union of love between people through the sacrament of marriage. But when it comes to marking parting and leave-taking, a time when some spiritual support is crucial, we are left bereft. No sacrament exists. Even further, the blatant silence here can mar us with useless and absolutely unnecessary shame or guilt. Even to this day, when I refer to myself as separated or divorced, a glazed look appears in people's eyes, particularly clerical ones. Shame on them!

Saying out that word 'divorce' is ugly and abrasive; a fifteenth-century French legal term for separation that needs updating. I would suggest that 'parting' is more realistic as in the Irish tune title 'Sgarúint na gCompánaigh', the parting of (one-time) friends.

Now, I stand beside people, mostly coming alone, in creating a new rhythm of meaning and purpose in their future paths. Although the word is cliché now, to seal and heal a 'closure' on their once-mutual affection through ritual is not simply a metaphor or symbol. It is a great and precious gift on two levels.

Firstly, it introduces an integration of the past to an identity for the future. Secondly, it bows and reveres the eternal depth to a partnership particularly when you create a family together.

Presence and meaning can live on through children and the narrative of that coming together continues on another level entirely. This is not the end, but the beginning; every breakdown is its own jump cable to restarting the rundown soul battery. When you have loved so deeply and parented with another person, it can take a long time – if ever – to give due attention and heal heart-breaking loss. Memories are always waiting to make the letting go harder and more painful. But remembering the good times is valuable and a keepsake of a love once lived and now transfigured.

A friend of mine, who separated painfully and with much hurt on both sides, once described to me the haunting that followed her. *'When I see him now, it's as if someone else is walking around in his old clothes.'* Stepping into that ritual space is the surest way to hasten the dawn of reconciling.

A ritual landscape recognises that this relationship in its former existence has run its course. The work is done. There is no room for anger, blame or resentment. Know that this is for your own good and this is your time to revitalise a life and to find hidden loveliness in the grace of the pain. Marriage 'till death do us part' is an outdated promise. Lifespans are now longer, and growing in tandem with someone for forty, fifty or sixty years is precious, but rare. Rather than hobbling through loveless, silent, angry nights, better to call it a day before each other, before others and before God. Rainer Maria Rilke puts it well: *'Be ahead of all parting … know what it is not to be … add yourself gladly and cancel the cost.'* (Sonnets to Orpheus II)

So let us pray on these following love-scarce snippets. Open your heart and soul to behold the sure knowledge that what you are experiencing in your heavy, hurt heart is carrying its own secret message and resolution. The revelation of this *Rún* (which means both 'love' and 'secret'), lies within yourself as you identify with some of the experiences of the following poets. They sat down in this bleak, lonesome chair under the same roof before you, desperately searching for words to console and identify their feelings.

I offer some prayers that I have found helpful to brighten the dawn of my own darkened days of shattered, fragmented hope and trust. Light two candles as you begin: one your own soul flame; the other for the person you have to let go their separate way.

Pause to trigger the good times and to give thanks. Another pause to call in the destiny of this moment and to acknowledge the Higher Force behind it all.

Recite the following Pushkin poem, aloud if you can. Then extinguish the once-lover's candle, remove it from your sacred space with a blessing of your own and carefully place it out of sight.

❋❋❋❋❋❋❋❋❋❋❋❋❋❋❋❋

Oh, I have loved you, and perhaps my spirit
Still harbours a warm glow of love today.
But God forbid that you be burdened with it:
I would not sadden you in any way.

I love you in a wordless, hopeless fashion.
Sometimes in jealous rage, sometimes struck dumb.
I loved you with a deep and tender passion.
May you be loved like this in years to come.
Alexander Sergeyevich Pushkin, 'I Have Loved You'

When the heart is broken, whatever the situation, the challenge is to emerge with dignity, a tranquil sense of yourself and, if at all possible, a smidgeon of gratitude for the new freedom awakened in you. David Whyte's *beannacht*, or benediction, carries within it such a graciousness and compassion for the one who perhaps wronged you or whom you wounded.

A blessing on the eyes that do not see me as I wish.
A blessing to the ears that can never hear the far inward
footfall of my own shy heart. Blessings to the life
in you that will live without me, to the open door
that now and forever takes you away from me,
blessings to the path that you follow alone and blessings
to the path that awaits you, joining with another.

A blessing for the way you will not know me
in the years to come, and with it, a blind outstretched
blessing of my hands on anything or anyone
that cannot ever come to know me fully as I am,
and therefore, a blessing even then, for the way I will
never fully know myself, above all, the deepest, kindest
wishes of my own hidden and untrammeled heart
for what you had to hide from me in you. Let me be
generous enough and large enough and brave enough

to say goodbye to you without any understanding,
to let you go into your own understanding,
to live fully in your understanding, and to gift
your understanding. May you always be
in the sweet, central, hidden shadow of my memory
without needing to know – who you were when
you first came – who you were when you stayed –
and who you will become in your freedom now
that you have passed through my life and gone.

David Whyte, 'Blessing for Unrequited Love'

❋·❋·❋·❋·❋·❋·❋·❋·❋·❋·❋·❋·❋·❋·❋·❋·❋

Ethna Carbery was an Irish republican poet and editor who died in 1902 at the age of thirty-seven. I love her poetry and although apparently happily married for just one year before her death, here is her *beannacht* or prayer for letting go. This I dedicate to my one time dear, now in his eternity of days. Mícheál Ó Súilleabháin. RIP *Tá a choineall múchta roimh bhreacadh an lae.*

❋·❋·❋·❋·❋·❋·❋·❋·❋·❋·❋·❋·❋·❋·❋·❋·❋

Our hands are met for the parting; your path must lie afar,
Yet well my heart shall know the way that leads to where you are,
And whether in gladness or in woe this is my prayer sincere –
The blessing of God be with you through all the day, my Dear.

May it be nigh you when the hours are filled with anxious care,
And guide you when the track of sin shows smooth and very fair,
May it ease your soul of every grief, scatter each cloud of fear –
The blessing of God be with you through all the day, my Dear.

The golden glory forsakes the sky, the throstle's song is dumb,
The flowers are sleeping on their stalks, and the parting time has
come;

It may be never again we'll stand in the gathered gloaming here –
Then the blessing of God go with you through all your days,
my Dear.
Ethna Carbery, 'My Prayer for You'

❋ ❋ ❋ ❋ ❋ ❋ ❋ ❋ ❋ ❋ ❋ ❋ ❋ ❋ ❋

BREOITEACHT: Heart Ritual in Times of Illness

As we bless our bodies, we thank them with great vulnerability daily. The slightest wince, stab of muscle pain when we rise, the nagging ache in the back that we all experience at one moment or another is enough to hurtle the neurotic mind down anxiety cul-de-sacs. Prayers have always been the best medicine, the prescription is free and never runs out.

My auntie Kit was a very holy woman. Elderly and infirm in a nursing home, she would say every time I visited, *'We're always begging God for something or other, especially when we are sick.'* And she is right – we turn to prayer in times of need. The Lebanese mystic, Kahlil Gibran, strongly and directly warned against this in his seminal work, *The Garden of the Prophet*: *'You pray in your distress and in your need; would that you might pray also in the fullness of your joy and in your days of abundance'*.

We pray when illness enters our house. It is terrifying when our fragile lives and hearts are confronted with serious sickness and no other person can really know what is going on for us. We have to grapple with infirmity on our own; sometimes we do it well, sometimes our altered world simply overwhelms us. Then, we turn to prayer to converse with the One who really knows and understands our psychological and physical pain long before its onset.

So now go to your *cúinne ciúin* – your quiet corner – sit, kneel, stand or lie down. Make yourself as comfortable as possible. I like to embrace my aching body at these times with a throw or blanket. Focus on the areas of your body that are complaining. Begin with your toes and travel up along the chakras that you have already met during your daily prayer stops.

Let your brain speak to your body. There is nothing to fear. This conversation, and your prayer now, have the power to ease your pain even if only by five per cent, slowly recite the following prayers.

❋❋❋❋❋❋❋❋❋❋❋❋❋❋❋❋❋❋❋❋❋❋❋❋

Thy name is my healing, O my God, and remembrance of Thee is my remedy. Nearness to Thee is my hope, and love for Thee is my companion.

Thy mercy to me is my healing and my succour in both this world and the world to come. Thou, verily, art the All-Bountiful, the All-Knowing, the All-Wise.

A prayer for healing from the Bahá'I tradition

❋❋❋❋❋❋❋❋❋❋❋❋❋❋❋❋❋❋❋❋❋❋❋❋

Tend to your sick ones, O Lord. Rest your weary one. Pity your afflicted one. Shield your joyous ones. And all for your love's sake.

Augustine of Hippo

❋❋❋❋❋❋❋❋❋❋❋❋❋❋❋❋❋❋❋❋❋❋❋❋

PAIDIR ROINNTE: Prayer Shared for Another in Sickness

Uniting ourselves with other suffering beings halves the isolation. As you have now focused on your own pain, just as in the Golden Rule on self-love, you are well poised to understand and empathise with other hurting souls.

Breathe gently and easily now for a few moments, closing your eyes. Now bring to mind the one who has asked for your prayers. A most caring prayer is uttered by Moses for his sister Miriam. She was stricken with leprosy after saying unkind things about him, yet he cried:

❁❁❁❁❁❁❁❁❁❁❁❁❁❁❁❁

Heal her now, God, I beseech Thee.
Numbers 12: 13

❁❁❁❁❁❁❁❁❁❁❁❁❁❁❁❁

This is a most powerful healing prayer and the second word can vary from 'me', 'her', 'him', 'them' or indeed 'the world'. This is a healing mantra and can be said over and over again.

Here is another Jewish healing prayer for a suffering one that I often turn to when people say 'pray for me'.

May the One who blessed our fathers, Abraham, Isaac and Jacob,
And our mothers, Sarah, Rebecca, Rachel and Leah,
Bless and heal this person [name]
The son/daughter of [mother's name]
May the Holy One, blessed be, be merciful and strengthen and
heal him/her
Grant him/her a complete and speedy recover – healing of body
and healing of soul.
Along with the ill, among the people of Israel and all
humankind,
Soon, hastily, without delay, and let us say: Amen
Mi Sheberach, For the Sick

IMNÍ ÉAGSÚLA: Prayers for Those who are Anxious, Worried or Fearful

Dark times bang on the door of every heart. Depression, loneliness, despair, hopelessness and doubt are just some of the sinister gifts that this visitor brings. There are many, many more. 'Dark times' is the umbrella term that embraces these life difficulties. Over and over again, in my overwhelming and chaotic hours, prayers come to the rescue. Not to banish the dismal feelings but to somehow ease the pain and help me to stand up again. The poets share and understand my blackness. Stumbling on the right prayer at the right time was a therapy in itself; even to believing that this was written just for me. My hope is that you will find this too in the following.

The little cares that fretted me.
I lost them yesterday
Among the fields above the sea.

Among the winds at play;
Among the lowing of the herds,
The rustling of the trees,
Among the singing of the birds,
The humming of the bees.

The foolish fears of what may happen,
I cast them all away
Among the clover-scented grass,
Among the new mown hay;
Among the husking of the corn
Where drowsy poppies nod,
Where ill thoughts die and good are born,
Out in the fields with God.
Elizabeth Barrett Browning, 'Fear'

ÉIGEANT ANDÚILE: Addiction

It is so easy to become addicted. Particularly when the dark clouds descend, we reach out in the wrong direction, we seek ease in obsessive habits to escape from the present moment. There seems no way to talk ourselves out into a new horizon of freedom. Our liberty is snatched from us, and our days are ambushed with obsessions and inner turmoil.

Yes, Ireland has had its fair share of addiction narratives. Most families, and mine is no exception, have their *scéal andúile féin* – their own dependence story. The nineteenth-century famines, subsequent emigration, poverty and dispossession were the lurking predators – Apostle Peter labels such devilish inflictions as '*a roaring lion waiting to devour*'. Fighting the demons, the temptations is another word for addiction.

'Addiction' is the amalgamation of *a* and *dicere*, to be without a say in our existence, to be literally speechless before our cravings and compulsions. An organisation, a broken promise, childhood trauma is enough to fan the destructive flame. The real tragedy is that in the compulsive habit, we lose contact with our relationship with ourselves and with the Higher Power. The addiction takes over. We have to hide this deep secret from others until the day dawns when we can emerge from the darkness knowing that we can move forwards.

Marijohn Wilkin's story is relevant here. The famous Gospel songwriter battled for a long time with alcoholism and drug abuse. Eventually, she turned to her religion for healing and marked it by writing one of the most famous ever Gospel songs, 'One Day at a Time, Sweet Jesus', where she asks God to show her the way one day at a time. Therein lies the saving mantra and gatha.

☀❀☀❀☀❀☀❀☀❀☀❀☀❀☀❀☀❀☀❀☀❀☀❀☀

God grant me the serenity to accept the things I cannot change,
Courage to change the things I can,
And wisdom to know the difference.
'Serenity Prayer'

☀❀☀❀☀❀☀❀☀❀☀❀☀❀☀❀☀❀☀❀☀❀☀❀☀

In the hour of my distress,
When temptations me oppress,
And when I my sins confess,
Sweet Spirit, comfort me!
When I lie within my bed,
Sick in heart and sick in head,
And with doubts discomforted,

Sweet Spirit, comfort me!
When the house doth sigh and weep,
And the world is drown'd in sleep,
Yet mine eyes the watch do keep.
Robert Herrick, 'Litany to the Holy Spirit'

❁⁂❁⁂❁⁂❁⁂❁⁂❁⁂❁⁂❁⁂❁⁂❁⁂❁⁂❁⁂❁

AMHRAS: Doubt

Indecision – or 'diddering' as my mother called it – is dangerous. At a crossroads in life, we wonder which is the 'Road Not Taken' as the poet Robert Frost writes about in his oft-quoted poem. In Ireland, we often say to define an uncertainly 'the answer is maybe and that's final' *(b'fhéidir - sin an fhreagra agus sin deire le sin)*!

❁⁂❁⁂❁⁂❁⁂❁⁂❁⁂❁⁂❁⁂❁⁂❁⁂❁⁂❁⁂❁

Lord, I believe, help my unbelief.
Mark 9: 24

❁⁂❁⁂❁⁂❁⁂❁⁂❁⁂❁⁂❁⁂❁⁂❁⁂❁⁂❁⁂❁

In *The Magnificent Defeat*, the American theologian, Presbyterian preacher Frederick Buechner, completes the doubtful plea with an air of certainty. *'Lord, I believe: Help my unbelief is the best any of us can do really, but thank God it is enough'.*

MAITHIÚNAS: Forgiveness

Below is one of the most striking blessings of forgiveness and generosity of heart ever written. When I offer this up, it fills me with the beautiful but difficult spiritual work of learning to pardon myself and others for failure of responsibility and the shame that it brings. May it do the same for you.

Gather yourself at your quiet altar of being. Bring in some music. Either play a recording or hum a tune. The eighth-century woman Islamic saint, Rabia, claimed that *'music helps to forgive'*. Try singing in forgiveness into your heart. As a singer, I know that it soothes the troubled soul. Humming is enough too.

A story from the Italian fourteenth century, St Catherine of Sienna, recalls that once, when she was navigating dark times, she sought advice from an old priest as to how to unburden her troubled heart. 'Hum your favourite tune,' he replied and all will be well.

❀✿❀✿❀✿❀✿❀✿❀✿❀✿❀✿❀✿❀✿❀✿❀✿❀✿

Bless all the hearts, the clouded ones, Lord, above all,
Bring healing to the sick.
To those in torture, peace.
Teach those who had to carry their beloved to the grave, to forget.
Leave none in agony of guilt on all the earth.
'To God, the Father' by Edith Stein, Sister Teresa Benedicta of the Cross

EASPA FUINNEAMH: Low energy

Scarcity of inspiration and energy visits us all. In my life, I often turn to the wisdom of the Book of Job at such times. A literary masterpiece of all time, the author paints an exquisite dramatic painting of the beauty of creation. A farmer and animal keeper, Job knows the sanctity of the natural world and indeed the human being. The beasts and the flora are our teachers; birdsongs are hymns; the low frequency sounds of fishes swimming have sacred secrets to impart. Be quiet, enough moaning; we must simply ask, and we shall receive if it be good for us.

But ask the animals, and they will teach you;
The birds of the air, and they will tell you;
Ask the plants of the earth, and they will teach you;
And the fish of the sea will declare to you.
Who among all these does not know that the hand of the Lord has done this?
In that hand is the life of every living thing and the breath of every human being.
Job 12: 7–11

UAIGNEAS: Loneliness

Loneliness has a doleful ring and meaning to it – the feeling of dejection, worthlessness, isolation and despair. Solitude on the other hand, defines a manner of living that we choose for ourselves.

People often ask me if living alone is lonely. I reply that it can be but that I usually see myself as solitary – akin to Wordsworth's solitary reaper singing to myself. When the call of lonesomeness beckons, I try, though I am not always totally successful, to cross the road as I see it approaching!

Loneliness has always been one of the sources of dark times – anxiety, depression and addiction thrive when people are lonely. Much research has been done on the profound parallels between loneliness and mental health. We, Irish, know a lot about it. In June 2023, ALONE, a national organisation to support the ageing, conducted the EU's first survey about loneliness and revealed that Ireland is the loneliest country in Europe. Everyone knows what this dark time brings. However, two things to remember here, as you bring your isolated self to pray: firstly, you are never alone in your isolation when you bring it to your altar of prayer and ritual; and, secondly, and in this order, *yours* is the choosing to remain or to go.

So, when lonesomeness descends, go to your quiet space, light the candle of connection to your heart and the world, speak out aloud your isolation and your fears. Pray for the courage to change and the strength this day to meet someone socially and to take a gentle nature walk if you can.

Jewish and Christian Scriptures are teeming with reminders that God is always with us. Buddhist wisdom teaches that when we welcome and embrace our solitude, we confront reality with all its uncertainties and fragility. Ritual is the bridge between both. We must nurture solitude.

※·※·※·※·※·※·※·※·※·※·※·※·※·※·※

Let nothing disturb you;
Let nothing dismay you:
All things pass;
God never changes.
Patience attains
All that it strives for.
You who have God
Find you lack nothing:
God alone is enough.
St Teresa of Ávila, sixteenth-century Doctor of the Church

※·※·※·※·※·※·※·※·※·※·※·※·※·※·※

Grant me the ability to be alone;
May it be my custom to go outdoors each day
Among the trees and grasses,
Among all growing things,
And there may I be alone,
To talk with the one that I belong to.
Rabbi Nachman of Breslov, cerebrated Jewish rabbinical
teacher and mystic of Eastern Europe

Alone with none but thee, my God,I journey on my way:
what need I fear when thou art near,
O King of night and day?
more safe am I within thy hand
than if a host should round me stand.
St Colmcille, sixth-century patron saint of Ireland

GO RAIBH MAITH AGAT:
A Ritual of Gratitude

'Thank you' in Irish is '*go raibh maith agat*', which means 'May goodness be yours'. When that little nasty voice of meanness, self-doubt, competition and limitation arises, I say, '*Go raibh maith agam*' – 'May goodness be with me'. Sometimes, a wholeness is restored as I bless myself – a lovely ritual – which physically has the power to shape our thoughts. When we say thank you, we are really saying 'I bless you'. We are shedding a sacred mantle of affection around the other.

Gratitude is an invitation to really treasure the grace that is present and correct in each moment.

A gratefulness ritual is most transformative at the dawning of the day. The morning is a great time to welcome the openheartedness of gratitude. Begin your day by summoning appreciation with the prayer of the English Anglican Samuel Johnson: '*Make me remember, O God, that every day is your gift and ought to be used according to your command.*'

The dew somehow cleanses our mind and showers it clean and free from the muddy waters of daily busyness and distraction; pure grace in itself.

'*In the morning, fill us with your love*', the scribe of Psalm 90 pleads. However, as we well know, it is the nature of our being to sink into diversions of thought and cul-de-sacs of interference, especially when we most try to avoid it.

Follow the recommendation of Trappist monk, Thomas Merton, who obviously went down this dead-end himself in his praying. Not only that, but he wrote that any prayer without disruption is not prayer at all at all. Leave guilt at the door. Let the internal commotion be. He says that the will to pray is the most important thing.

A ritual of gratitude is a verb; it does something to both the giver and receiver – similar to forgiveness, both have the word 'give' inherent in them – thanks – giving and forgiving.

*Thanks*giving is all about our being in union – union, comm*union* with each other and with the ultimate Other. The essence of Thanksgiving Day is spiritual. So often, people exhale in relief or ecstasy – '*Oh Thank God*', '*Thanks be to God*'. Perhaps the best known and most often quoted gratefulness wisdom of Meister Eckhart is: *'If the only prayer we ever said was thank you, that would suffice.'* Thanksgiving is our nature and grace. In other words, we are fully alive when we appreciate the world and others around us. When we get out of the *'glass-bottles of our ego'* as D.H. Lawrence put it and when the 'me' becomes 'we'. The Divine dwells completely in the ease of grace.

When we say yes, we are opening ourselves up to the other. When we complain, we turn away from gratitude.

Dag Hammarskjöld reminds us: '*For all that has happened, thanks; for all that will be, yes.*' Gratitude, consent and welcoming the future are, therefore, one and the same when it comes to understanding time and space. For the past, with all its griefs, worries and woes, we say 'thank you' with a breath of relief that what has passed has passed! For the future, with all its uncertainties, we gingerly whisper yes and, for the present moment, we simply pray!

Do not become hardened and closed in on yourself. If we somehow can live in kindness and gratitude, we will be surprised by heart warmth, imagination and possibility. An ungrateful heart houses a wizened, unfulfilled life.

Below is a Hindu gratefulness or homage prayer that I have in my prayer book since my first visit to India in 1982. That image of the 'Breath of Life', that divine respiration is one very powerful image of all prayer. A Sufi prayer is held together by two strands of thread: listening and breath.

❀✲❀✲❀✲❀✲❀✲❀✲❀✲❀✲❀✲❀✲❀✲❀✲❀✲❀

Homage to you, Breath of Life, for the whole universe obeys you. You are the rule of all things on earth, and the foundation of the earth itself.

Homage to you, Breath of Life, in the crashes of thunder, and in the flashes of lightning. The rain you send gives food to the plants and drink to the animals.

Homage to you, Breath of Life, in the changing seasons, in the hot dry sunshine and the cold rain. There is comfort and beauty in every kind of weather.

The plants themselves rejoice in your bounty, praising you in the sweet smell of their blossom. The cattle rejoice, praising you in the pure white milk they give.

Homage to you, Breath of Life, in our breathing out and breathing in. At every moment, whatever we are doing, we owe you praise and thanksgiving.

Homage to you, Breath of Life, in our birth and in our death. In the whole cycle of life you sustain and inspire us.

Homage to you, Breath of Life, in the love and friendship we enjoy. When we love one another, we reflect your infinite love.

Men and women rejoice in your bounty, praising you in poem and song. The little children rejoice, praising you in their innocent shrieks of laughter.

Atharva Veda (5.2.23)

One of the most comforting prayers I know is from the Book of Lamentations, which is widely attributed to the prophet Jeremiah. The highlight for me in the midst of this rather forlorn, despairing Old Testament tome appears in Chapter 3: 'The steadfast love of the Lord never ceases, his mercies never come to an end: they are new every morning; great is your faithfulness'. (Lamentations 3: 22–23)

What an encouragement and resilience is St John of the Cross. Persecuted by his own fellow priests, he endured such torture and humiliation and, yet, his one desire was to be still and to live out his life free from spiritual anxiety and despair.

Give me stillness of soul in You. Let your mighty calmness reign in me. Rule me, O King of Gentleness, King of Peace. Give me control, great power of self-control, control over my words, thoughts and actions, from all irritability, lack of meekness, lack of gentleness, dear Lord, deliver me. By your own deep patience, give me patience. Make me in this and all things more like you.
St John of the Cross

Close your ritual of thanksgiving now by relaxing those fifty-two muscles in your face until you banish that frown. When I am truly grateful, I love to dance! Try it! Clear a little space. As for help in choosing the steps as Mechtilde of Magdeburg prayed. In her book *The Flowing Light of the Godhead*, she says that she cannot dance until God teaches her which will bring her to the sacred circle of ritual where she will remain forever.

The ritual motto here is the Buddhist practice of wearing half a smile constantly, apparently as the Buddha bore.

AG DUL IN AOIS AGUS BÁS:
Ageing, Dying and Death

Ageing gracefully, as the cliché puts it, is all about our grace to rise above anxiousness as best we can. Turning to God is the greatest Tao – way – to free ourselves, transfigure and transform these inevitable burdens of ageing and death fears. The English feminist novelist, Winifred Holtby, believed that while we journey through this finite, passing world, it is our vocation well lived that will save and give meaning. '*God, give me work till my life shall end and life till my work is done.*' *The oldest collection of Buddhist women's prayers is the Therigatha, two thousand year old verses from 'elder nuns'.* Psalm 24 describes the elation which scaling the heights of emancipation from frailty guarantees.

Though I be suffering and weak, and all
My youthful spring be gone, yet have I come
Leaning upon my staff, and clambered up
The mountain peak.
My cloak thrown off,
My little bowl overturned, so sit I here
Upon the rock. And over my spirit sweeps
The breath of liberty! 'I win. I win.'
The Triple Lore! The Buddha's will is done!
A Jewish promise from the Divine:

And I will still be carrying you when you are old. Your hair will
turn grey and I will carry you. I have made you and I will carry
you.
Isaiah (Chapter 46)

After you have taken the time for healing prayer, here is a fragment of a very rich spiritual reflection on sickness as a portal to the next life. This is the liminal time when our celestial candle is now flickering weakly before the blowing out and the advent of the perpetual flame of eternity.

Since I am I to that Holy roome,
Where, with thy Quire of Saints for evermore,
I shall be made thy Musique; as I come
I tune the Instrument here at the dore,
And what I must doe then, thinke here before.
John Donne, 'Hymne to God, My God, in My Sickness'

CLEACHTA SNÁITHE: A Thread Ritual to Soothe the Bothered Heart

In every life, there are moments of chaos and crisis when we lose our way forwards. The path ahead fades into the mists or divides into so many forks in the road that we harden and stop almost dead. How will we launch out into the lonesome voyage of the future? This is a time for the great challenge of new beginnings. Rituals hold the key to the pilgrimage through the 'vale of tears' or, as William Butler Yeats coined, '*the hollow lands and hilly lands*'.

Jewish Scriptures teaches that there is a proper time and season for every experience, including grieving and despair, which too shall pass. A '*time to weep*' gives way to '*a time to laugh'*. Providence is listening to *'every purpose/activity under the heaven'* (Ecclesiastes 3) waiting in the wings to provide the perfect antidote.

The silent ritual is this. Find a ball of wool or a reel of thread and cut a piece roughly the length of your arm. Find a quiet space to restore the soul's equilibrium. In the absence of a sewing kit, a hair band, ribbon, tie, cord, a shoelace or elastic band.

With thread in hand, remind yourself that every new beginning must emerge from some letting go to allow space for an epiphany, a propitious moment that suddenly waylays and transforms. Part of the course of living well is to learn to recognise and welcome, not only the new path but also the bid farewell to the death, the completion of one another, usually repetitious, dependency that is holding us back.

In the Christian tradition, Mary, Mother of God, is the one who listens tenderly and takes the focus from you yourself, offering to be the untier of knots for you. This is her gift and promise to you and to the world. An ancient belief, it was way back in the first century that St Irenaeus awakened this image of Mary, the undoer of knots. The first earthly people, one creation story tells us, were Adam and Eve. It is the latter that is blamed for all of life's sorrows, apparently through her disbelief and disobedience. However, there was a pair of them in it who together tied the universe up in knots; Mary, the new Eve in faith, is releasing them since with perfect Divine symmetry, rhythm and proportion.

Now slowly wind that thread into a ball as you say – out loud if you choose – and heed the advice of two poets named William. The Kansas poet and pacifist, Stafford, directs you to grasp your dream cable and never let go; Blake's invitation promises a spiritual pilgrimage amidst the vast diversity of this carefully woven pathway to the celestial. Here is the string but you must play your part by winding it up first and then the gate of transformation opens wide before you; the New Jerusalem Gate.

Sit or stand quietly now, slowly turning in your hand your unrolled orb of thread as you mull over your anxiety which could be suffering, aloneness or loss. Wait for the nudge to unravel it as you release the tangled clusters to its former horizontal identity. As every bunch of chords is different, so too is the unravelling of each soul's struggles.

❊❈❊❈❊❈❊❈❊❈❊❈❊❈❊❈❊❈❊❈❊❈❊❈❊

There is a thread you follow. It goes among
Things that change. But it doesn't change.
People wonder about what you are pursuing.
You have to explain about the thread.
But it is hard for others to see.
While you hold it you can't get lost.
Tragedies happen; people get hurt
or die; and you suffer and get old.
Nothing you do can stop time's unfolding.
You don't ever let go of the thread.
'The way it is', William Stafford

I give you the end of a golden string
Only wind it into a ball
It will lead you into Heaven's gate
Built in Jerusalem's Wall.
William Blake, excerpt from 'Jerusalem'

SIÚIL AGUS GUÍ:
To Walk is to Pray

Up until now, we have focused on prayer at an altar and the creation of a sacred space indoors. But nothing is more sacred than nature and it is the perfect place for prayer.

For me, walking is the ultimate ritual. Almost every day, I head up to the forest of Glenstal Woods near where I live. It brings me great joy, sensing the beauty and indeed the privilege of being alive. For the hour and a half that my walks take, my ears embrace the world of sound, air and earth, and a new sense of adventure and possibility becomes the centre of my being.

The flawless path is always ambulated, according to the Spanish mystic John of the Cross, *'the way of perfection is not travelled by flying but by walking'*.

Since time immemorial, walking has been one of the most salubrious movements enjoyed by humanity. Hippocrates, the Father of Medicine, was the first to emphatically pronounce this some 2,500 years ago: *'Walking is man's best medicine. Woman's too!*

The irony is that, in going out for a walk, we are most often treading into another inner heart path. Go out with a problem and walk home with the answer. Leave the crisis behind on the path.

St Augustine identified this. The Latin phrase *'solvitur ambulando'* – it is solved by walking – is attributed to him. Now, this once-wild young man is very careful not to specify *what* is resolved through the walk. So, this counsel is always your own. Only you – and the Divine – know what your deep heart's core needs are at this moment.

Augustine sang as he went, as I do too. For he is credited with the directive to *'sing and keep walking'*. Many self-help programmes prescribe walking for a calmer mind, sturdier bones, back pain relief, glaucoma, eye-disease prevention, the onset of dementia, and so on. The Danish philosopher Søren Kierkegaard concurred with this contemporary research. Over a 150 years ago, he shared: *'Every day I walk myself into a state of well-being and walk away from every illness.'*

Then, there is the social aspect of walking with a companion. Sometimes, we can easily lose the motivation to get out on the path alone. Make a date with a friend to share the road and the load is halved. Side by side, stories and secrets are swapped. We say in Irish '*gioraíonn beirt bóthar*' – a road shared is a life compared. And not simply for story sharing, education for the early Greeks was all about walking up and down; Aristotle apparently at once walked, talked and taught. The nineteenth-century German philosopher Nietzsche also taught on foot, believing that '*only thoughts reached by walking have value*'. The imagination is whetted when we step it out. When I was trying to integrate, bring together and articulate a theology of listening, on many occasions, the well of creativity ran dry. One morning, when I was faced with a crossword-like dilemma, I needed a term to embrace and capsulate the heart of the matter of Divine listening; the silence of God, the voice of God, how to hear and interpret that voice, the sound of God, the ear as the perfect spiritual sense, etc. My ritual when such bland impasses descended, was to hit for the high hills for a spell; rosary beads in hands to plead for inspiration. It nearly always worked and certainly did this afternoon. Seemingly from nowhere – although that place doesn't exit in spiritual terms – the penny dropped with the till-then secret title of *theosony*. Walking awakens sleeping thoughts and inspiring ways.

It is the spiritual nature of walking that an ambulatory ritual seeks to explore. For Henry David Thoreau, who wrote a classic walking book, the experience was akin to the religious, which is coming home to oneself in the midst of solitariness. The following observations are crucial.

❋❋❋❋❋❋❋❋❋❋❋❋❋❋❋❋❋❋❋❋❋❋❋❋

I come to myself, I once more feel myself grandly related, and that the cold and solitude are friends of mine. I suppose that this value, in my case, is equivalent to what others get by churchgoing and prayer. I come to my solitary woodland walk as the homesick go home ... It is as if I always met in those places some grand, serene, immortal, infinitely encouraging, though invisible, companion, and walked with him ... It comes only by the grace of God. It requires a direct dispensation from heaven to become a walker ... Heaven is under our feet as well as over our heads.

❋❋❋❋❋❋❋❋❋❋❋❋❋❋❋❋❋❋❋❋❋❋❋❋

Seamus Heaney captured this very manner of walking the earth though perhaps more from a pragmatic rather than a spiritual impulse or intention. Keep your feet firmly grounded. Keep your eyes looking ahead.

Movement is body, somatic prayer, a very delicate form of prayer and exquisite expression of worship. Never the teaching or sharing of the church alas; the body is only from the head up. Anything could happen is something I always remind myself of before taking that first step. This could be the most important moment in my life so, please God, let me be open to risk and your providence.

AN SIÚLÓID LEIGHIS: The Healing Gait

This walking and listening ritual is for yourself and on your own. No distraction from the business at hand, which is to extol the senses and let them bless you. Meister Eckhart, the German Dominican mystic, makes a visual observation that works as well if not better for the roaming ear: *'The ear by which I listen to God is the same ear by which God listens to me'*.

Stroll outside now alone and listen as you step it out. First become aware of the cosmic sounds around you, your own feet falling on the ground, the cattle, the breeze through the trees, the distant sound of traffic above and below: Cosmic theosony, I call this. Birdsong is all around.

Birds are simply not just our feathered friends; they are our profound teachers and role models for life. Sing, when the first light of day peeps through, fly, to warmer climes when the winter appears, the early bird catches the worm, build your nest safe from harm, and so on. However, the real lesson, according to poet Terry Tempest Williams, is when we look to them as teachers of prayer.

Next, wake to the gift of this moment. Offer thanks for the blessing of mobility. Know that, at this time, the surprise insight is waiting to ambush you out of the ditch. This is *theosony* with a message. But now you may graduate on to the point where every step becomes a prayer. Commit the ambient noises and the shock of the surprise attack of wisdom completely to a Higher Force and you now walk in Silent Theosony where the very walking is a sacred ritual and the simple power of everyday prayer.

The natural world is a window into the divine for so many ancient cultures. The world around us is a visible sign of an invisible grace. Let us conclude our walking pilgrimage with an original, very early utterance from the Irish tradition.

※❋※❋※❋※❋※❋※❋※❋※❋※❋※❋※❋※❋※

Achainím ort tríd an uisce, Is tríd an aer glan anfach, Achainím ort tríd an tine, Achainím ort tríd an talamh.

I beseech you in the name of water and through the stormy, crisp air. I invoke you through fire and I entreat you through the ground beneath.
Tenth-century hymn

※❋※❋※❋※❋※❋※❋※❋※❋※❋※❋※❋※❋※

NA FÉILTÍ CEILTEACH:
The Celtic Year of the Wheel

The Celtic soul put great store on the ever-turning cycle of seasons. Like the omnipresent God, every day is new, vibrant, changing and dynamic. This ancient circle of seasonality is as old as humanity itself when at the very beginning, each season was the vital and essential possession of the goddess and each of the four Celtic seasons celebrated some aspect of the feminine. Each one begins on the eve of the first day of the months of November, February, May and August – in Ireland, we like to do things differently! So instead of following the norm of celebrating the two Solstices and two Equinoxes, the Celtic mentality surprises by taking the midpoint between all four stations of the sun.

Thus, *Samhain* is celebrated between the Autumn Equinox (21 September) and Winter Solstice (21 December); *Imbolc* falls between 21 December and the Spring Equinox (21 March); *Bealtaine* follows between Spring and Summer Solstices; *Lughnasa* equidistant from 21 June to Autumn Equinox.

The names of the seasons come from old Irish names: *Samhain* means the end of summer; *Imbolc,* in the belly time of fertility; *Bealtaine* meaning either the mouth of the fire or named after Belenus, the God of the sun; and Lughnasa called after the God of the harvest, Lugh.

Celtic time revolves around this quartet of feasts and the annual progression of light from darkness into brightness. Imbolc to Lunasa, including Bealtaine, stretches between the bright solar stations of Spring through to the end of Summer – whereas the short days and longer periods of nightfall encompass Samhain to Imbolc, also the first day of Spring in Ireland.

This circle of blessing and belonging to this four-fold cycle is filtered down through the ages to us today through this prayer. Let it set the backdrop for our ritual of cyclical recognition.

❋❋❋❋❋❋❋❋❋❋❋❋❋❋❋❋❋❋❋❋❋❋

Bail ó Dhia ort ó Shamain to lá le Bríde, ó lá le Bríde go Bealtaine,
ó Bhealtaine go Lughnasa agus ó Lunasa go Samhain.

The blessings of God be with you from Samhain to Brigid's Day
from Brigid's Day to Bealtaine, from Bealtaine to Lughnasa and
finally from Lughnasa back to Samhain.

☀·☀·☀·☀·☀·☀·☀·☀·☀·☀·☀·☀·☀·☀·☀·☀

SAMHAIN: Winter

Samhain marks the beginning of the Celtic Year and celebrates
the wise old woman, the *cailleach*. Believed to be the oldest of
the festivals, it is time set apart for honouring the ancestors:
the departed and Samhain go hand in hand. We are now in
the dead of winter when the deceased return to bless us and
stay awhile where they once lived. Black is the colour of the
dark, again the most ancient shade from which all others were
born.

In mythological literature and poetry, a shade refers to the ghost
or spirit of a dead person now dwelling in the Underworld.
The short spans of the sun and the moon during this season
must have been such a rare blessing and gift to be named the
'Face of God'. Black is the visible sign of mourning. Everyone,
in times past, including the priest presiding over the funeral
service, wore black clothing.

Death is an individual, a persona, in Irish consciousness. The irony is that we know death to be alive and a person, always a man, that visits without warning. One time in Kerry when I was collecting traditional religious songs from older singers, the conversation turned around to death. Seán de hÓra was the conversation partner and he wistfully looked away and said, '*Is fear díreach é an bás; ní chuireann sé scéal ar bith roimhe*' – Death is a blunt, dangerous character; he never tells you when he is going to call. And you have no choice but to open up when he knocks on your door as the following proverb cleverly puts it: '*Ní féidir dul i bhfolach ar an mbás*' – There is no hiding place from father death. Because death is always before us, walking beside us, we have no fear of that ultimate journey.

Firstly, we must trust that when that presence comes to our front door, if we have done the best we can and lived our lives in kindness and love, then we will exit this world in prayer and peace. Secondly, we are coming home not solely to our own profoundest soul at last, but to that divine presence that has always been the invisible companion in life. Prayer and mindful ritual are the soul-rhythms. In an old prayer attributed to St Bridget, she assures us that she will make Heaven 'a cheerful spot' where the inhabitants will be imbibing from a great lake of beer 'and every drop' will be a prayer – and ritual too! As a neighbour of ours long go used to say, 'Sure, Heaven must be great fun, because no one ever came back!'

RITE SÍNSEAR SAMHAIN: *Samhain Ritual*

The feast of Samhain is a very powerful season; a metaphor for ageing, death and ancestral remembrance. Therefore, throughout this seasonal span, bringing this season back home through ritual is vital and the key to the Celtic tuiscint or understanding.

Firstly, create your own Samhain altar. Mark it apart with black fabric. Place ancestral photos there and surround the images with three candles: one honours our ancestors who have passed over; one for our present families who are living; and the third for those who will come after us.

Go outdoors and gather some fallen leaves. Name each one as you place it on the Samhain altar as some dark emotion that you want to heal at this time: anger, grief, loneliness, sadness, despair and trust.

Samhain is presided over by *An Cailleach Bhéara* – the Celtic goddess and first woman's voice in Ireland. Now in the Samhain of life, she has learned one ultimate life-lesson. Her final insight: *'All I know is how to die – and I'll do it well.'* Pray now for yourself; for the virtues of poise, dignity and humour as you advance in years. Secondly, earnestly seek to speak with your beloved past ones. As Kahlil Gibran reminds us, there is no surer way to converse in a transformative way with our loved ones save through prayer: *'When you pray, you rise to meet in the air those who are praying at that very hour, and whom save in prayer you may not meet.'* Weave into this ritual a blessing of your ancestry now.

Place three candles at your altar space. Light the first candle, which symbolises our family lineage.

❊❊❊❊❊❊❊❊❊❊❊❊❊❊❊❊❊❊❊❊❊

I bow my head and give honor and thanks to my immediate blood family – to my mother and father, my grandmothers and grandfathers from whose flesh and blood I am created. I welcome their energy, their wisdom, joys and sorrows in me, and I genuflect before all our roots and heritage. In the lighting of this family ancestral candle, I am expressing my gratitude to you for tending the land for me, for creating a home for me, and although that sanctuary was mostly safe and comforting, I am letting go, as best I can, the times when that land and hearth was not harmless and secure. But you did work as hard as you were able to create a better world not simply for me but for others around.

May you support, guide and protect me through your silent presence and whisperings, both of which are as audible and as constant as the quiet beating of my heart.

❊❊❊❊❊❊❊❊❊❊❊❊❊❊❊❊❊❊❊❊❊

Light the second candle which honours our Spiritual ancestors.

❋⁂❋⁂❋⁂❋⁂❋⁂❋⁂❋⁂❋⁂❋⁂❋⁂❋⁂❋⁂❋

*I am now bowing to my spiritual intimates, to all those who
have turned me towards the good in so many seen and unseen
ways. My teachers and mentors along my path of growth, who
taught me unknown to myself. I honor those who are yet to enter
the days and years ahead to grace me with their perceptions
and insights. I honour the great mystics, Christian and other
faiths, who inspired me, I think of Christ, Mary, Anna and I
am promising to continue to live out their message of love and
compassion from this day forward. I am remembering with
great forgiveness the fore parents who hurt me and wounded me
along the way, the dark associates who because of their own pain
passed that on to me and slowed me down on many occasions.
I pray for their peace and I do not want them to continue to
suffer. May you now support, guide and protect me. Everything
that I have received I want to share and give back to my lines
in the future. I want to say only what will be wholesome and
nurturing for the children to come.*

❋⁂❋⁂❋⁂❋⁂❋⁂❋⁂❋⁂❋⁂❋⁂❋⁂❋⁂❋⁂❋

Light the third candle which symbolises my successors to
come, the descendants yet to be born.

Spend a quiet moment now before you extinguish the
candles to let any memories, happy or sad, settle in your soul.

IMBOLC: Spring

Imbolc salutes the spring and the young pre-puberty girl, the *Brídeóg*. The Celts were a pastoral tribe, people of the land and hailing the passing of the unfarmable winter was a wonderful relief. The youngest of the seasons, we pray for new beginnings, new dreams and possibilities, perhaps, to take a new path in our life's purpose. To be in the flow is a good image now as snows are thawing and rivers are gushing down the mountains in this time of year. The surge of a river is always teaching us; be graceful, to trust in the path, to dance to the rhythm of your being and divinity. Authenticity and truthfulness are the hallmarks of the water course and of Imbolc. Water is a purifier. Now is a time for inner and outer spring cleaning.

RITE IMBOLC: Imbolc Ritual

Prepare your Imbolc altar upon a bright-green background. Adorn it with some wild spring flowers that you have gathered. A bowl of water nearby for you to irrigate these blossoms and spring clean your soul. Now ask yourself the following *coicead* – a cluster of five questions – for you to put to your heart jury this Imbolc. Give your heart plenty of time to reply with the answer that you need to hear:

- What is the new beginning you long for in your life?

- What wisdom are you seeking as you emerge from hibernation?

- What message do you wait to hear and what changes will that entail?

- What lessons are others seeking to tell you?

- What have you been struggling with and are complacent about and long to abandon?

Green is the colour of growth and spring energy. Winter darkness bows to welcome in the new emerald blades of grass and leaves dancing in the trees, sporting their costumes of forty shades of green. I remember one of my father's manners of speech describing someone was 'ah, he's a little green' meaning that he was naïve, inexperienced and gullible. A little daub of this nuance is perhaps not a wholly bad trait either; sophistication and superficiality can rob the heart of wonder and awe.

A prayer to heighten our Imbolc ritual. Patrick Kavanagh, the Monaghan poet, was a prayer poet of God. Of his over 250 poems, over 130 are about the divine presence which he lived and breathed in through the earth and in the natural world. May we too come alive in Imbolc to first observe, then to know, the angel of the peaks: '*I lift up my eyes to the mountains …*' (Psalms 120)

O give me faith
That I may be
Alive when April's
Ecstasy
Dances in every
Whitethorn tree.

O give me faith
That I may see
The angel of
The Mountainy
Places in dream's
Infinity.
Patrick Kavanagh, 'A Prayer for Faith'

BEALTAINE: Summer

Walking is the ritual celebration of May Day, more clement weather beckons us out into the open air. Longer evening and earlier mornings mean that we have no excuse. Red, the colour of blood, life forces such as anger and, of course, the Christian Holy Spirit is the characteristic colour. Bealtaine is the creative season of the fertile young woman, walking into independence and relationship – the *Bábóg*. A time to walk the land, deiseal, clockwise, sprinkling it with the first well water gathered that morning of the 1st May.

The four cardinal directions were saluted by a brief pause and a reverential bow to each. The beasts of the field were blessed by making the sign of the cross on their backs. Walking to holy wells, a ritual of all the Celtic feasts, carrying out the three stations or rounds of the well. Leaving an offering, ensured good health and prosperity. Bealtaine morning dew was collected in a jar and rubbed onto the face to maintain youthfulness and good looks and to banish the particularly Irish facial feature of freckles! (The source of all contemporary cosmetic skin tonics and moisturisers!) I often heard my mother and her sisters share their childhood memory of the negative destiny that would befall a household if a robin flew into the house on Bealtaine; some member would pass over shortly.

Fires, again, a ritual in all feasts, were ignited and cows were driven in between two stations of fire for protection against disease before they were herded into the high pastures. *'Idir dhá thine Bhealtaine'* is an old saying meaning 'between the two fires of Bealtine'. People, too, sometimes walked through for the same longing and passion for continued safekeeping. Even daring, flamboyant young men would leap over them for fertility during the coming year.

RITE BHEALTAINE: *Bealtaine Ritual*

A Bealtaine ritual assumes aspects of walking, water and fire. Walking, to praise the earth and human connection to it. Water, the mother and source of life – to bathe our face in its primeval vitalism. Fire the symbol of forgiveness and release to shape the contours of the creative path of change. Bealtaine is the season to at one and the same time, walk the earth and touch the divine. Our Bealtaine – mouth of the fire – ritual is an imaginary visualisation around the *tine* (fire).

Close your eyes. Imagine a Bealtaine bonfire; we are all sitting around it and visualise those flames now in your mind. What are the colours? Is it blazing or smoky? Listen to the crackling of the burning wood. Be aware of that wholesome odour of wood. Feel the heat of its warmth. Watch the bright-red flames, born out into the air and sky. It is warming. Feel the heat on your hands, feet, face.

Now let us invite this energy of fire/sun into the body. Beckon that fire energy towards you and assure it that it will be welcome. Listen now to what that creative energy of the glowing crimson blaze has to say to you. Are you sensing the presence of another in the centre of this flame? Someone you know who has become a shade or someone you desire to speak with now through the energy of the glow. An old wound that is ready to fuel the flare of release.

In your own time, send that energy back to its source, thanking it for visiting and being the messenger at this moment. Now come back to your breathing – in and out. Give yourself a body embrace, feel the touch of your hands on your face and on your body.

❋❋❋❋❋❋❋❋❋❋❋❋❋❋❋❋❋❋❋❋

Let us ask for healing through walking, fire and water, the pillars of Bealtaine. As we gently turn the wheel of the year towards the gifts which this feast promises, may we know that we are always journeying from darkness towards light, from night towards dawn, from death towards immortality.

❋❋❋❋❋❋❋❋❋❋❋❋❋❋❋❋❋❋❋❋

LUGHNASA: Autumn

The season of harvesting and maturity completes the perfect circle of Celtic time; the presence of the mother, the nurturer, the harvester is welcomed. Lughnasa lends perspective to the process of journeying from birth to death in our lives. Now we can gather in, glance at our own image of ourselves. As we age, we can learn to see our memories, regrets and lost achievements as destined moments that have brought us here to this Lughnasa mellowing. The motto here is from two lines of poetry that say it all. A little poetic, genderistic licence might allow its subtle presence to hover nearer.

*No man needs to be a mediocrity, if he accepts himself as God
made him. God only makes geniuses.*
Patrick Kavanagh

To paraphrase, whatever way we look at it, each one of us is
one with the divine – a work of God's hands.

Ageing is often synonymous with wisdom; we have crossed
the threshold; the grain has been separated from the chaff.
Upon the wheel, we have embraced our darkness and now we
are awakening to the presence of light as we are called again,
to spiral out, carrying our medicine bundles of this year's
experiences and teachings. What are we ready to leave behind,
so we may participate, fully and wholly, in the vibration of our
Mother Earth's song of rebirth? Her beat is strong, our pulse
vibrates to her nature. Listen now. She is calling us to waken.

Rust – that magnificent mélange of orange and brown – is
surely the colour of Lughnasa. I first appreciated the grace of
this autumnal shade one late-autumn day. I was presenting
with my sons, at the wonderful Yoga Centre, Kripalu in
Stockbridge, Massachusetts. Mícheál, my youngest son,

had spotted that there would be a henna tattoo artist that afternoon. Off we waddled, not knowing what might be ahead of us. A wonderful experience which added such a colourful dimension to our performance that evening. My hands glowed with this intricate pattern set in a very subtle russet. Over the course of the two weeks that it graced the back of my hand, this rust skin signature was almost like a divine face smiling up at me daily. I missed it when it faded – as you would a friend who had just left.

RITE LUGHNASA: Lughnasa Ritual

Take a comfortable posture. Begin to focus around your 'heart centre', breathing in and out from that area. Next, evoke a kind feeling toward yourself. 'God only makes geniuses'; remind yourself of Kavanagh's radical claim. Drop beneath any areas of self-judgment or self-hatred to the place where we long for and discover strength, health and safety. Continuing to breathe in and out, use either these traditional phrases or ones you choose yourself. Say or think them over several times.

❋✻❋✻❋✻❋✻❋✻❋✻❋✻❋✻❋✻❋✻❋✻❋✻❋

May I be free from inner and harm and danger. May I be safe and protected through the season.

May I be free of mental suffering or distress as I draw inspiration and healing from the cycle of time.

May I be happy and in the deep sense of that word, may I be the happening of happiness for others.

May I be free of physical pain and suffering and in my health and strength, live my life in this world peacefully, lovingly and at ease.

❁❁❁❁❁❁❁❁❁❁❁❁❁❁❁❁❁❁❁❁❁❁❁❁

Next, move to a person who motivates you toward love and repeat the above blessings for them.

❁❁❁❁❁❁❁❁❁❁❁❁❁❁❁❁❁❁❁❁❁❁❁❁

May she/he be free from inner and outer harm and danger …

❁❁❁❁❁❁❁❁❁❁❁❁❁❁❁❁❁❁❁❁❁❁❁❁

Now, repeat the phrases for someone you struggle with, who challenges you.

If you have difficulty doing this, you can say before the phrases, 'As best as I can, I am sending you a blessing. As best as I can, I know that the virtues that I find uneasy in you are some shadow traits of my own. I pray that I may learn from this experience with you and I wish you well.' Abide in silence for a few more breaths, then journal about your experience, if you are moved to do so.

To conclude, landscape outlasts us. The seasons which we have blessed and just honoured will come and go for thousands of years after we have gone. Hand in hand with the seasons – you can't have one without the other – is the mystery all around us that we call Nature. In Ireland, we talk of someone we really admire as 'being full of nature'. A great compliment indeed.

FOCAL SCOR :
The Last Word

But today, well lived,
makes every yesterday a dream of happiness,
and every tomorrow
a vision of hope.
Look well, therefore, to this day.
Ancient Sanskrit proverb

The virtues of faith, hope and love appear under various guises in most religions. The first and third have dominated but really hope is a braided thread that secretly and silently recurred over and over again in this tapestry of sacred ritual. Entering the ritual altar, which we have created already together, is one giant step of expectation. To pray is, in one sense, to hope.

'I hope and pray ...' we often say in Ireland. Hope precedes and urges prayer. It is never prayer before hope. It is as though hope knows where and when to pray when you need it. It reclaims and restores us for the path, the Tao, ahead.

The human soul, particularly during these present times – torn asunder by despair and anxiety – is thirsting for confidence and certainty of purpose. We now have a clear insight into the two-fold source of all contemporary crises; the lack of the spiritual and quotidian ritual and the absence of hope. Our traditional institutional structures have collapsed into the sand and no longer provide us with safe secure foundation.

Although we may be on the brink of despair on so many fronts, all is not lost. With no turning sideways and no establishment to reach out to, sacred ritual holds the secret everyday resolution. The irony is that the emptiness and desolation can be traced back to our turning our backs on prayer. In the media, politics, economics, family and community life, prayer and its ritualistic expression is ridiculed as naïve and laborious, outdated God-stuff. Whereas the exact opposite is true: a repossession is the sacred which brings a maturity of wisdom and a newness of life that is hidden in the deep recesses of our unconscious. Which is why I use the term 'repossession'.

As we take our leave from each other's company, there are two underlying messages of this book of prayer: one is that you are not alone in this; others have gone before us. Our ancestors, the mystics have already provided the signposts. Yet, it would be a great mistake to limit the world of prayer to the mystic. For, prayer, ritual and blessing belong to everyone. The motto is *not* that the pray-er is a special kind of person but that every person is a special kind of pray-er.

Secondly, although you now know my way of being at home in ritual, you will have your own way of being in prayer – customs, practice and behaviours – that I have never thought of at all. May you discover hundreds of ways to express this and add your own habits of existence and growth.

The ultimate questions of the heart that haunt us are heard and answered through prayer. Sooner or later, we must give way to this wisdom that's been garnered from many ancient insights – a tiny glimpse which I have presented here.

Ireland is the source and the cradle for such a prayer revolution. This is no castle in the sky, no naïve or romantic theory. Ireland somehow and still remains detached from the rest of the world. Come here and you step into another world. Apart from its visible residents and occupants, the ground below is eternally shimmering – *ag biorradh*, is the sweet sound in Irish. Echoes of all of our ancestral millions, are faintly to be heard in the stone circles, the rocks, the prehistoric tombs, the ever-flowing waters. The layers of surface beneath have been carefully preserved and maintained.

The genius *loci* of the land continues to enable the spirit of people, place and the Divine to thrive and flourish. That is when connection to the deep spirit of ritual declares itself and draws us near to whisper in our souls.

This is a time of spiritual zeitgeist, a defining period in the history of cosmic spirituality. Ritual is the unique expression and remedy to the dark side of the coin we live in; *Sacred Rituals* is a spiritual zeitgeist book.

Then, of course, there is the invisible realm – our nearest neighbours – always looking out for us. *Muintir na Sí, na daoine maithe*, whom we affectionately name the good people are close family; principle actors and no extras in the zeitgeist drama. Geniuses at praying before us, these intimate spirits, goddesses, gods, saints and scholars, are reweaving that cloak of between-ness and connection, alive, expanding and offering the world hospitality and freedom through hope and prayer. This force promises to keep our lives vital, daring and welcoming. In a word, we, Irish, like being world trailblazers and we are good at it.

Below are the three final appreciations and blessings

Firstly, prayer activates your imagination and in so doing reminds you of the course from which you came from. Unique to you, the excavating is also yours.

Secondly, ritual helps us to fulfil our life's purpose, to sprinkle us with meaning, and hope.

May the prayer in your heart feel and guide you in the wonder of your mysterious worth and steadfastness through sacred ritual.

Thirdly, and most importantly, a life of prayer, ritual and blessing rests in the mind of God, The Higher Source and Power, the ultimate destination of our souls; prayer is our trusted though most oftentimes ignored *anam-chara* (soul friend).

On the journey, may some ritual within these covers bring you into unity with your own grace, which is your own invisible sign of the visible Divine. May a language of prayer shape your words and worlds into a forgotten, or yet undiscovered, mother-tongue.

Now that this prayer tome has grown up and left home to enter yours, I say farewell to it now as it finds whoever needs it, a literary Good Samaritan. May this book be a source of ritual, grace and inspiration from a surprising source.

May it, little book of my heart, never return home but fall into the hands of all who need it.

Thank you, reader, for coming on this journey with me!

Rath Dé ort go deo!

Nóirín

Iúil 11 Lá Fhéile Benedict, 11 July, Feast of St Benedict. Guru Purnima – July festival to express gratitude to spiritual teachers.

AGUISÍN:
PAIDREACHA BREISE:
Appendix: Added Prayers

Here are some additional prayers you may wish to use for your special intentions:

PRAYERS ON LIGHTING THE ALTAR CANDLE

'Set your love before me as a light!
A candle tall; so shall I, weak, prevail
O'er Darkness; pass beyond all venomed things
Into the endless Dawn, gold-starred, rose-pale.'
Ethna Carbery 1864–1902

MORNING PRAYERS

Éirimis le Dia is le Muire is le Pádraig. An Té a chuir an oíche aréir tharainn go dtuga sé cabhair is cúnamh chun an chuid eile den lá a chur tharainn.

Let us arise with God, with Mary and with Patrick. May the
one who saved us through last night help and protect us to spend
the rest of the day wisely.
Traditional prayer from Lios Mór

You are ushering in another day, untouched and freshly new
So here I come to ask you, God, if you'll renew me, too?
Forgive my many errors, that I made yesterday,
And let me try again, dear God, to walk closer in your way.
Father, I am well aware that I can't make it on my own
So take my hand and hold it tight for I cannot walk alone.
Helen Steiner Rice 'Good Morning, God!'

EVENING PRAYERS

'We thank thee, Lord, for the glory of the late days and the
excellent face of thy sun. We thank thee for good news received.
We thank thee for the pleasures we have enjoyed and for those we
have been able to confer. And now, when the clouds gather and
the rain impends over the forest and our house, permit us not
to be cast down. Let us not lose the savour of past mercies and
past pleasures; but, like the voice of a bird singing in the rain,
let grateful memory survive in the hour of darkness. If there be
in front of us any painful duty, strengthen us with the grace of
courage; if any act of mercy, teach us tenderness and patience.'
Robert Louis Stevenson, 'Prayers at Vailima'

SILENCE

'Be still and know that I am God.' (Psalm 46:10)

TRUST

'A low prayer, a high prayer, I send through space; Arrange them yourself, O God of Grace!' Scots Gallic proverb

'Know that I am always with you even to the end of time.'
(Matthew 8:20)

'Pray in private, shut the door – Aramaic threshold.'
(Matthew 6:6)

'O Lord, you search me and you know me,
You know my resting and my rising…
You mark when I walk or lie down,
All my ways lie open before you.'
(Psalm 139)

A BLESSING TO SHARE

'May the Lord bless and protect you.
May the Lord make its face shine upon and be gracious to you;
may the Lord turn her face toward you and give you peace.'
(Numbers 6)

'In your mercy heal us, in your love and tenderness remake us. In your compassion bring grace and forgiveness. For the beauty of Heaven may your love prepare us.'
(Anselm)

DISCERNMENT
'Here I am! Send me.'
(Isaiah 6:8)

'No devotee of mine is ever lost. Take refuge in me and you reach the highest goal.'
(Bhagavad Gita IX 31-32)

'Do your work, then step back. The only path to serenity. Those who know don't talk, those who talk don't know. Wanting to reform the world without discovering one's true self is like trying to cover the world with leather to avoid the pain of walking on stones and thorns. It is much simpler to wear shoes.'
Rama Maharshi

ILLNESS
'Thus says the Lord: "Stand at the crossroads, and look, and ask for the ancient paths, where the good way lies; and walk in it, and find rest for your souls."'
(Jeremiah 6: 16)

'Om! Earth, Sky, Heaven.
We meditate on the brilliant light of the Sun.
May it illuminate our minds!'
(Rig veda 3.62.10)

'So do not fear, for I am with you; do not be dismayed, for I am
your God. I will strengthen you and help you; I will uphold you
with my righteous right hand.'
(Isaiah 41:10)

'O Lord, thou knowest how busy I must be this day:
If I forget thee, do not thou forget me.'
General Lord Astley (1642)

ALTÚ BÉILE – MEALTIME GRACES
'Those who are cheerful and merry at table will benefit from
their food.'
(Ecclesiasticus/Sirach 30)

Bless, O lord, before we dine,
Each dish of food, each glass of wine
And Bless our Hearts that we may be
Aware of what we owe to Thee
Nineteenth-century Leather sellers' anthology

We thank thee Lord for this our food, and that we are together.
(Mennonite Prayer)

May all who share these gifts today
Be blessed by Thee we humbly pray.
Be the meal of beans or peas,
God be thanked for those and these.
Have we flesh or have we fish
All are fragments from God's dish
Robert Herrick, d. 1674

Go, eat your bread with enjoyment and drink your wine with
a happy heart for God has long approved what you do.
(Ecclesiastes 9)

Bless our meal, Dear Lord, bless us all, each one of us, and let
us find among pain and joy that you have lit your peace in our
home.
J.J. Bondesen (1844-1911), Danish fairytale writer

Bail ar na gcúig arán agus an dá iasc a roinn Dia ar na gcúig
mhíle fear.
Rath ón Rí a rinne an roinn go dtaga sé ar ár gcuid agus ar ár
gcomhroinn
May the five loaves and two fish that God divided among the

five thousand be blessed. May the blessing from the King who
divided descend upon our food and upon our sharing.
Míle buiochas dhuit, a Thiarna Dia:
An té a thug go bheatha seo dúinn
Go dtuga sé an bheatha dár n-anamacha
Más fearr atáimid inniu,
Go mba seacht bhfearr o bhéas muid blain ó inniu.
Slán I ngrá Dé agus I ngrá na gcomharsan,
I dtrócaire agus I ngrásta, I saol agus I sláinte.
(A thousand thanks to you, O Lord God. You are the one who
gave us life, the one who gave life to our souls. If we are blessed
today, may we be blessed seven times more this day next year.
May we be safe in the love of God and the love of our neighbors,
in mercy, in grace, in life and in health.)
Ár bPaidreacha Dúchais, Diarmuid O Laoghaire SJ, Baile
Atha Cliath, 1975 36, 46 trans. N.Ní Riain

Lord, to those who hunger, give bread. And to those who have
bread, give the hunger for justice.
Native Latin American

LOVE

If I speak in the tongues of men and of angels, but have not love,
I am only a resounding gong or a clanging cymbal. If I have the
gift of prophecy and can fathom all mysteries and all knowledge,

and if I have a faith that can move mountains, but have not
love, I am nothing.
St Paul (1 Corinthians 13:1)

I am the Bridegroom, Love, you are the bride
Mountains of cinnamon surround our wedding bed.
Love me until the wild world's tears are dried
Set me like a seal, my love replied
Priests in the temple of the body take this bread
You are the bridegroom, love, I am the bride.
Even when now and then our worlds collide
Passion flowers striped and peonies blood red
Love me until the wild world's tears are dried
Nothing can break this bond once we decide
To weave it round our hearts with scarlet thread
I am the bridegroom, love, you are the bride
Strolling through gardens where love was denied
Old age won't find these sap-filled branches dead
Love me until the wild world's tears are dried
Bodies inside a tomb identified
As man and woman intertwined, they said
I am the bridegroom, love, you are the bride
Love me until the wild world's tears are dried
Mark Patrick Hederman OSB 1999, 'Abbot'

ADDICTION

Enlighten me with a clear shining inward light, and remove all darkness from my heart. Repress my many wandering thoughts.
Thomas à Kempis (1380–1471)

DOUBT

O give me faith
That I may be
Alive when April's
Ecstasy
Dances in every
Whitethorn tree.
O give me faith
That I may see
The angel of
The Mountainy
Places in dream's
Infinity.
Patrick Kavanagh , 'A Prayer for Faith'

DEATH

A transition perception by Pierre Teilhard de Chardin, French Jesuit and philosopher, who wrote 'we are not human beings having a spiritual experience; we are spiritual beings having a human experience'. A salubrious thought as we muse on death and dying.

When the signs of age begin to mark my body (and still more when they touch my mind);
When the illness that is to diminish me or carry me off, strikes from without, or is born within me. When the painful moment comes in which I suddenly awaken to the fact that I am ill or growing old; and above all, at that last moment, when I feel I am losing hold of myself and am absolutely passive within the hands of the great unknown forces that have formed me. In all these dark moments, O God, grant that I may understand that it is you who are painfully parting the fibres of my being in order to penetrate to the very marrow of my substance and bear me away within yourself.
Teilhard de Chardin, 'Le Milieu Divin'

Fear of death is directly related to a loss of self-purpose and vocation.

I have life left with me still
And thy purpose to fulfil;
Yea a debt to pay thee yet:
Help me, sir, and so I will.
Gerard Manley Hopkins, Excerpt from 'Prayer'

Tagore on 30 July 1941, on the day prior to a scheduled operation; his final poem.

I'm lost in the middle of my birthday. I want my friends, their touch, with the earth's last love. I will take life's final offering, I will take the human's last blessing. Today my sack is empty. I have given completely whatever I had to give. In return if I receive anything – some love, some forgiveness – then I will take it with me when I step on the boat that crosses to the festival of the wordless end.

The Book of Job is one of the most sensible and shrewdest Scriptures from the Judaeo–Christian texts. The aged Job eventually acknowledges the wisdom and strength that God's presence in our lives promises. Here are two Jobian prayers that remind us of this.

'Is wisdom with the aged, and understanding in length of days?'
(Job 12: 12)

'Let days speak and many years teach wisdom.'
(Job 32:7)

THE REALITY AND CELEBRATION OF DEATH

Our beloved dead are always with us, many many cultures remind us and their presence is particularly recognised in Ireland. A theosonic singing in our ears, as the Lebanese–American writer and poet, Kahlil Gibran, believed.

'I shall live beyond death, and I shall sing in your ears
Even after the vast sea-wave carries me back
To the vast sea-depth.
I shall sit at your table though, without a body,
And I shall go with you to your fields, a spirit invisible.
I shall come to you at your fireside, a guest unseen.
Death changes nothing but the masks that cover our faces.
The woodsman shall be still a woodsman.
The ploughman, a ploughman.
And he who sang his song to the wind
Shall sing it also to the moving spheres.

His epitaph which is beside his grave:
'A word I want to see written on my grave:
I am alive like you, and I am standing beside you.
Close your eyes and look around, you will see me in front of you ...'
Kahlil Gibran, *The Garden of the Prophet*

CHAPTER 15 THE BHAGAVAD GITA

For to Him come they
From passion and from dreams who break away;
Who part the bonds constraining them to flesh,
And – Him, the Highest, worshipping always –
No longer grow at mercy of what breeze
Of summer pleasure stirs the sleeping trees,

What blast of tempest tears them, bough and stem:
To the eternal world pass such as these!
Another Sun gleams there! Another Moon!
Another Light – not Dusk, nor Dawn, nor Noon –
Which they who once behold return no more;
They have attained My rest, life's Utmost boon!
On the day I die, as my casket is being carried away,
Don't think it pains me to leave this world.
Don't weep for me; don't wail 'Alas'
Don't fall into the devil's snare, that would be sad indeed.
When you see my cortege, don't say, 'He's parting!'
For me, it is the moment of meeting and reunion.
As you bury me in the earth, don't say, 'Good-bye!'
For the grave is a veil over union in Paradise.
When you see the lowering down, think of the rising up.
When did setting ever lessen the sun or the moon?
What seems a setting to you is but a rising.
The tomb may seem a prison, but it is freedom for the soul.
What seed is buried in the ground and doesn't grow?
Why therefore do you doubt this human seed?
What bucket is lowered and doesn't come up filled?...
When you close your mouth on this side, open it on the
Other and let your song echo through the air of the void.

Jalaluddin Rumi, Divan-I Shams – Tabriz 911

The nineteenth-century poet Christina Rossetti had a great sense of celebration of the unrestricted soul in death:

When I come to the end of the road
And the sun has set for me
I want no rites in a gloom filled room
Why cry for a soul set free?
Christina Georgina Rosetti, excerpt from 'Let Me Go'

Rabindranath Tagore penned this funeral verse giving thanks for a life well-lived:
'Farewell, my friends.
It was beautiful
As long as it lasted,
The journey of my life.'

WALKING
There are additional nature poems here that reveal the inner secrets on the divinity of the natural world.

Great Spirit Prayer
Oh, Great Spirit,
Whose voice I hear in the winds
and whose breath gives life to all the world.
Hear me! I need your strength and wisdom.

Let me walk in beauty, and make my eyes
ever hold the red and purple sunset.
Make my hands respect the things you have made
and my ears sharp to hear your voice.
Make me wise so that I may understand
the things you have taught my people.
Let me learn the lessons you have hidden
in every leaf and rock.

Translated by Lakota Sioux Chief Yellow Lark in 1887

Oh God, enlarge within us the sense of fellowship with all living
things, even our brothers and sisters the animals, to whom you
have given the earth as their home in common with us. We
remember with shame that in the past we have exercised our
high dominion with ruthless cruelty so that the voice of the
earth, which should have gone up to you in song, has been a
groan of pain.

St Basil, fourth century

Lord, may we love all your creation, all the earth and every
grain of sand in it. May we love every leaf, every ray of your
light.

Fyodor Dostoyevsky, *The Brothers Karamazov*

O, King of the Tree of Life,
The blossoms on the branches are your people,
The singing birds are your angels,
The whispering breeze is your Spirit.
O, King of the Tree of Life,
May the blossoms bring forth the sweetest fruit,
May the birds sing out the highest praise
May your Spirit cover all with his gentle breath.

Celtic Prayer

NÓTA BUIOCHAIS: ACKNOWLEDGEMENTS

My gratitude lies with my family, initially my father and mother, my beloved sister, Marion, who passed over some months ago, Stephen and the Flynns, Noel, the best brother ever, Annette and the Ryans and all my ancestors.

My sons, Owen and Mícheál, who never lost faith in me.

Owen nudged me persistently and this book would not be here without him. *Mo mhíle buiochas*, Eoin.

My daughters-in-law Andrea and Namu, and my grandsons, Finn Riain and Arún were inspirations to Mamó to complete.

Creating and experiencing the power of sacred rituals with so many people, in marriage, death and grief, one-to-one spiritual counselling, since my ordination in 2017, convinced me of the urgent need for such a resource. Furthermore, our hundreds of pilgrims on our Turas d'Anam journeys here in

Ireland were willing trial groups and are eagerly awaiting its birthing.

Just when motivation was scarce, Ciara Doorley from Hachette Ireland miraculously appeared, along with her competent team of Joanna Smyth, Claire Rourke, Stephen Riordan and the entire Hachette Ireland crew. I am grateful beyond words for their sound editorial advice and various inputs.

Integral to the direct content were: Alice Peck, Abbot Mark Patrick Hederman OSB, Professor Patricia Kieran and Keith Kristich.

Soul friends/*Anam Cháirde:* Marie Richardson and Mary Condren, soul daughters/*anam iníonacha*, Kathrena and Annette Ryan, and Neasa Ní Argadáin. Aryeh Maidenbaum and Diana Rubin, are dear Jewish chaverim.

Soul healers during the writing were Ralph Quinlan Forde, Francis Lanuza and Anna Gibson Steele. Anne O'Connor, my dear neighbour, supplied delicious brown bread and marmalade throughout, and Tina Rainsford tended to the home space.

Two monastic communities have taught me the truth of the ancient maxim: *Bis orat qui cantat* – the one who sings prays twice. The monks of Glenstal Abbey have been my spiritual teachers for over fifty years; Simon Sleeman and Colmán Ó Clabaigh were directly supportive. The Cistercian sisters of St Mary's Abbey, Glencairn, were always there for me.

Two wise world shapeshifters, poet David Whyte and theologian Matthew Fox, continue to inspire me both personally and spiritually.

Four gurus whose earthly candle has been extinguished and are now showering down blessings on the good of it all: Mícheál Ó Súilleabháin, John O Donohue, Seán Ó Duinn OSB and Ciarán Forbes OSB.

Tá a gcoinnle múchta roimh bhreacadh an lae.

Finally, thank you, reader, for taking that first courageous step into the mansion of ritual, blessing and prayer; the path is here, it's yours and is already cleared before you.

PERMISSIONS ACKNOWLEDGEMENTS

NOTES

NOTES

NOTES

NOTES

NOTES

TREOIR-LEABHAR : INDEX